Lourdes Today

A Pilgrimage
to Mary's Grotto

KERRY CRAWFORD

SERVANT
BOOKS

PUBLISHED BY FRANCISCAN MEDIA
Cincinnati, Ohio

Cover design by Candle Light Studios
Cover photo by Tentencents Photography
Interior design by Mark Sullivan

LIBRARY OF CONGRESS CATALOGING-IN-PUBLICATION DATA

Crawford, Kerry.
Lourdes today : a pilgrimage to Mary's grotto / Kerry Crawford.
p. cm.
Includes bibliographical references.
ISBN 978-0-86716-825-9 (pbk. : alk. paper) 1. Christian pilgrims and pilgrimages—France—Lourdes. 2. Lourdes (France)—Religious life and customs. 3. Christian shrines—France—Lourdes. 4. Mary, Blessed Virgin, Saint—Apparitions and miracles—France—Lourdes. 5. Lourdes (France)—Church history. I. Title.

BT653.C68 2008
232.91'7094478—dc22
                                    2007043065

Published by Servant Books, an imprint of
Franciscan Media
28 W. Liberty St.
Cincinnati, OH 45202
www.FranciscanMedia.org

Printed in the United States of America

To Patricia and James Crawford,
Carol and Jim Crawford, Trish Crawford

CONTENTS

. . • . .

chapter one

. • .

BERNADETTE AND THE LADY

It was an unlikely story from the start. Bernadette Soubirous, a very fragile fourteen-year-old child, left her home on Thursday, February 11, 1858, with her sister, Toinette, and a friend, Jeanne Abadie. The "home" in question could hardly be called that. It had in earlier times served as the jail or *cachot* for Lourdes, a village of four thousand tucked in the foothills of the French Pyrénées. The prisoners had deserted it decades before for better, more sanitary living conditions.

André Sajous, a stone mason, and his family occupied one floor. Sajous's workshop was on the lower floor, along with a room that his own family had rejected as unlivable. This room, what had been the *cachot*, now lodged the Soubirous family of six, including parents François and Louise Castérot, their daughters Bernadette and Toinette (eleven) and their sons Jean-Marie (six) and Justin (three). Dark and humid, the room opened to a small courtyard piled with dung in which a privy overflowed. The stench was overwhelming.

This place was a last resort for the Soubirous family—a lifeline Sajous tossed to his cousin Louise and her husband. Taking up residence in the *cachot* was proof to all that François had hit rock bottom.

François and Louise had known better times. As newlyweds the couple lived in the Boly Mill along the Lapaca, a stream that flowed into the River Gave. Remembered later by Bernadette as the Mill of Happiness, it was both home and workplace for Louise's family of origin. Her marriage to François brought the Castérots a son-in-law to replace her miller father, who had died in an accident.

Louise, who at eighteen was about half the age of François, gave birth to Bernadette in an upper bedroom of the mill on January 7, 1844. The baby was baptized Bernarde-Marie Soubirous two days later on her parents' first wedding anniversary in the Church of St. Peter. Like her Aunt Bernarde, for whom she was named, Bernadette entered the world as "the heir," a recognition given by custom in the Pyrenean county of Bigorre to the firstborn son or daughter.

When Bernadette was eleven months old, a fire from a candle enveloped Louise's blouse while she dozed. As a result of her injuries, Louise could no longer nurse her baby. She sent her to Marie Laguës in the village of Bartrès to be wet-nursed. Bernadette did not return home for ten months.

While Madame Castérot, Louise's widowed mother, kept the books and oversaw the mill accounts times were good. Her departure with her older children in 1848 gave the young Soubirous family more independence, but she took with her the discipline needed to run the mill profitably. At the same time, flour mills driven by steam were changing the landscape of industry and displacing skilled men like François Soubirous. A milling accident blinded

François in his left eye and made him even less employable.

With the decline of business and increase in expenses, the die was cast. In 1854 the new owners of the Boly Mill evicted the Soubirous family when they could not pay the rent.

Other events of the time made the dire circumstances of the Soubirous family worse. A cholera epidemic swept through Lourdes in the fall of 1855. More than three dozen people died, and many others were left diminished, including eleven-year-old Bernadette. She would never fully recover her health. Famine followed in 1856. The government distributed free flour, eliminating any work François could hope to find.

In order to keep the family fed, François Soubirous became a *brassier,* a day laborer who rented out his arms *(les bras)* and muscle. Louise worked as a field hand or did housekeeping to help supplement the family's income. Even Bernadette contributed. In the winter of 1856–1857, she kept house for her Aunt Bernarde and tended the family's bar. Between September 1857 and January 1858 she worked as a shepherdess and servant for her former wet nurse in Bartrès.

But the family's collective efforts fell short. There was no money for rent. Thus the *cachot,* a twelve-by-fourteen-foot room, became home.

A home, however, is more than its walls and roof. A home is also measured by the love within it. By this yardstick the *cachot* was not found wanting. Every night the Sajous family heard the Soubirous family below them praying to God. Other accounts indicate that the family was united in love and faith.

On the rainy morning in question, Louise reluctantly gave her blessing to Bernadette and Toinette to go with their friend to search for firewood. Louise had hesitated about Bernadette. Chronic asthma and bronchitis, resulting from her bout with cholera, all too often robbed Bernadette of breath. But Toinette and Jeanne, the mother figured, would do most of the work. If the girls were successful, the firewood could be sold to the ragpicker for a few pennies, enough to put a pound of bread on the table. Placing a patched white hood, called a capulet, on Bernadette's head, Louise said good-bye to her daughters and Jeanne.

Leaving the *cachot* at 15 Rue des Petite Fossés, the three girls headed to the outskirts of Lourdes. They crossed the Pont Vieux, "the Old Bridge," spanning the River Gave de Pau, then turned right and crossed the canal that supplied the local Savy sawmill with water. On a suggestion from Bernadette, they headed through the fields to the point where the canal and the River Gave joined. Bernadette now faced the front of a rocky cliff with a cave carved out of its bottom, the Grotto of Massabielle.

Toinette and Jeanne removed their wooden shoes and waded through the icy millstream to scavenge for sticks and bones on the opposite bank. Remembering her mother's warning not to catch cold, Bernadette hesitated. She called out to her companions to help her throw stones in the water so that she could cross over without removing her shoes, but the two would have none of that.

Resigned, Bernadette started to take off her shoes and stockings. It was then that she heard a noise "like a gush of wind" coming from the grotto. Glancing behind her at the River Gave and the meadow, Bernadette was surprised that the branches of the poplars had not budged. She bent over and continued to remove her stockings. Once again she heard the noise.

Bernadette looked up and saw some wild rose brambles stir in the niche above the grotto. A soft light brightened the recess. And within that halo of light, Bernadette saw a girl about her age dressed in white. A blue sash hung at her waist. A yellow rose adorned each bare foot. The mysterious young lady smiled at Bernadette.

"When I saw that, I rubbed my eyes," Bernadette would later recount. "I thought I was mistaken."[1] It was no mistake. Bernadette could not rub away the image of the young girl. Now fearful, she reached into her pocket for her rosary. She attempted to make the Sign of the Cross with the crucifix, but she could not lift her hand to her forehead.

The young girl in white lifted her own rosary with its white beads and blessed herself. No longer afraid, Bernadette tried again to do the same and this time succeeded. As Bernadette said her rosary, the young girl in white fingered the beads but did not move her lips during the *Aves*. She vanished when Bernadette finished her prayers. This was the first of eighteen meetings Bernadette would have with the mysterious girl, whom she would later come to realize was the Blessed Mother of God.

Wondering what she had just encountered, Bernadette finished removing her stockings. She crossed the millstream, which was surprisingly warm, and caught up with Toinette and Jeanne. She immediately asked them what they had seen. Neither had seen or even heard anything unusual. Promising not to whisper a word to anyone, Toinette pressed her older sister to tell all.

The secret was out the moment the Soubirous girls carried the firewood into the *cachot*. Toinette rushed to report that Bernadette had seen a girl in white in a cave. Louise promptly paddled both girls and forbade Bernadette to return to the Grotto of Massabielle.

Bernadette, however, could not stay away. Three days later—and a day after telling her first confessor, Father Pomian, about what she had seen—Bernadette felt drawn to Massabielle. Her confidence buoyed by her father's permission to go and armed with a bottle of holy water, she led a group of her curious classmates down the path to Massabielle.

The young lady in white did not disappoint. When she appeared Bernadette sprinkled holy water on her while praying, "If you are from God stay, but if not, go away."[2] The young lady smiled and stayed.

As before, only Bernadette saw the apparition. When she finished praying the rosary, the young lady disappeared. So intent, though, was Bernadette's communion with the beautiful girl that her friends could not move her from the spot. They ran to the sawmill and enlisted a brawny young miller to help pull her back up the footpath.

Word spread like wildfire through the village. Soon Louise Soubirous arrived with a stick in hand. She had to be convinced not to beat her pale daughter, whose cheeks were just regaining some color.

The last thing Louise Soubirous wanted in their small hometown was a scandal. A little less than a year before, gendarmes had arrived at the door of the *cachot* and carried away François. Unjustly accused of stealing two sacks of flour, he spent nine days in prison. This embarrassment, combined with the shame of living in the *cachot*, still stung. With so little in their favor, Louise did not want the eyes of the community on her family. The worried mother again drew the line. Bernadette was not to return to Massabielle.

Holding that line was an altogether different story. Jeanne-Marie

Milhet, a former servant who had acquired some wealth by marrying her employer, was intrigued by the unfolding story of the apparitions. Strangely convinced that the vision might, in fact, be the late Elisa Latapie, a relative of Milhet known for her virtue, she was determined to learn more.

Madame Milhet had a bargaining chip to get what she wanted. She was one of the few women who hired Louise Soubirous for odd jobs. Louise gave in and allowed Bernadette to go to the grotto with Madame Milhet and her dressmaker, Antoinette Peyret, in the early morning of February 18. Once at the grotto, the three began the rosary.

"She's here," Bernadette told the others, who could not see the lady. After they finished praying, Antoinette pushed paper and pen toward Bernadette. As Madame Milhet had coached her to do, Bernadette, who could not read or write, stepped forward and held the paper and pen up to the niche.

"Would you be kind enough to write your name down?" she asked. The young lady in white smiled and spoke for the first time in the local dialect. "It is not necessary," she said. She then asked Bernadette a question, "Would you have the kindness to come here for fifteen days?" Bernadette promised she would. The lady in white offered a pledge of her own: "I do not promise to make you happy in this life but in the other."[3] The apparition, whom Bernadette knew for certain was not Elisa Latapie, vanished.

Carrying a borrowed blessed candle, Bernadette kept her appointments at the grotto for the next three days. During each visit, witnessed by an increasingly larger circle of family members, friends and the curious, Bernadette knelt transfixed before the lady. Onlookers witnessed only the frail Bernadette in ecstasy, her rosary in one hand and the candle in the other, staring at the cavity in the rock, moving her lips and at times pausing, as if she were listening.

The activity at Massabielle did not escape the attention of the town elders. After the sixth apparition on February 21, police commissioner Dominque Jacomet brought Bernadette before him. Questioning her alone, Jacomet established that Bernadette Soubirous did not know how to read or write, seldom went to school, had not made her First Communion and, in fact, did not even know if she was thirteen or fourteen. She admitted forthrightly that her mother, aunt, sister, friends and even the nuns had doubted her story. Yet this uneducated girl, so without guile, could not be swayed from her story. She was convinced that she had seen *Aqueró*, meaning "that one" or "that thing" in the local dialect.

Jacomet was frustrated. Rumors were flying in Lourdes and beyond, some even suggesting that the Blessed Virgin was appearing to this nobody. Taking his written notes from the interview, he played with the facts, twisting what she had said in order to trap her. Bernadette countered his creative fiction at every turn. No, she said, she had never claimed to have seen the Blessed Virgin—"you've changed everything," she said.[4]

At the end of the day, the police commissioner had failed to get what he wanted most from Bernadette: a promise not to visit the grotto again. She explained that she had already pledged to return. This was a promise she intended to keep in spite of the commissioner's threat to jail her.

The next time the lady appeared to Bernadette, on February 23, she told her some things that were for Bernadette alone. These are traditionally held to be three secrets, which Bernadette never revealed. On February 24, the eighth apparition, the gathered crowd saw Bernadette go into the grotto, walk on her knees and kiss the ground. A sad *Aqueró,* Bernadette later said, asked her to do this as penance for sinners. "Penance, penance, penance," the apparition said to Bernadette. "Pray to God for sinners."[5]

On February 25 the lady visited Bernadette again and asked, "Would you kiss the ground for sinners?... Would you eat the grass for sinners?" She told Bernadette, "Go drink at the spring and wash yourself there."[6]

Bernadette's first impulse was to move toward the River Gave, the only apparent source of water. Stopping and appearing puzzled, she reversed direction and returned to the grotto. There she scraped the ground until she drew some muddy water out of the earth. Cupping it, Bernadette raised her hand to her lips, drank and then spit the water out.

"*Aqueró* told me to go drink at the spring and to wash in it. Not seeing any spring, I went to drink at the Gave; but she beckoned with her finger for me to go under the rock," Bernadette recounted later. "I went and found a little muddy water, almost too little for me to hold in the hollow of my hand. Three times I threw it away, it was so dirty. On my fourth try, I succeeded."[7]

Bernadette not only drank the muddy water but also smeared some on her face. Then she ate the leaves of a wild plant. Many of those witnessing the spectacle wondered if the poor child had lost her sense. It now was easy to dismiss this simple miller's daughter, who left the grotto escorted by her embarrassed aunts. But later that day the water started trickling and then flowing clear from the hole Bernadette had dug.

While the uncovering of the spring raised new questions, Bernadette's behavior at the grotto fanned the flames of suspicion among the town officials. That night Vital Dutour, the imperial prosecutor, interrogated her and threatened her with jail. While his intimidation got the better of Bernadette's mother, the girl would not recant, nor would she promise to stay away from the grotto.

The next day, February 26, Bernadette prayed her rosary at the grotto and repeated the strange acts of penance. The beautiful girl did not appear, and Bernadette wondered if she had offended her. This setback did not prevent Bernadette from returning to Massabielle and humbling herself in the same way as the lady had earlier requested. The tenth, eleventh and twelfth visitations of the young lady occurred February 27 and 28 and March 1.

March 2, the day of the thirteenth apparition, brought a crowd nearing two thousand and a new request. The beautiful lady told Bernadette, "Go tell the priests that people should come here in procession and that a chapel should be built here."[8]

With her Aunt Bernarde and Aunt Basile at her side, Bernadette presented herself to Father Peyramale, the authoritative pastor of St. Peter's Church. She explained that *Aqueró* wanted people to come to the grotto in procession. The pastor sized up Bernadette, a slip of a girl, mostly illiterate about her faith. It was too much. Go home, he ranted, and do not return to the grotto.

Within hours Bernadette was back at the rectory. She had forgotten to mention, she explained to Father Peyramale and the other curates that the lady wanted a chapel built too! Father Peyramale demanded that Bernadette ask the lady her name.

When the lady appeared to Bernadette on March 3 and again the next day, she smiled but did not comply with the parish priest's request. As an added credential, Father Peyramale now insisted that the lady make the wild rosebush blossom in the winter grotto.

Without this evidence there would be neither a chapel nor processions. A large crowd came on March 4, hoping for a final revelation, but they left disappointed. This was the last of the original fifteen visits.

Life returned to normal, as much as it could for the fourteen-year-old. Having kept her promise to meet with the lady fifteen times and deliver the message to the priest, she no longer felt the urge to visit the grotto. Bernadette struggled to learn her catechism in preparation for her First Communion.

As Bernadette tried to sleep the night before the Feast of the Annunciation, she experienced an inner call to return to the grotto. Before the sun rose on March 25, she and her parents made their way to Massabielle. They were surprised to find a crowd already gathered there in the hope that the feast day would bring renewed blessings and favors.

For the sixteenth time the lady appeared. Knowing what Father Peyramale required, Bernadette dared to ask four times, "Mademoiselle, would you be good enough to tell me who you are?" Slipping the rosary over her right arm, unfolding her arms, extending them toward the ground and then folding them at her breast, the lady raised her eyes to heaven and finally answered, "*Que soy era Immaculada Councepciou,*" "I am the Immaculate Conception."[9]

Although the words were in her own dialect, they were foreign to Bernadette. Relieved that she now had a name to tell the priest, she worried that she might forget what the lady had said. All the way to the pastorate of Father Peyramale, she repeated the strange words over and over again. Standing before the priest, Bernadette named at last the one who had been nameless: "I am the Immaculate Conception."

The astonished priest wondered how this uneducated girl, whose catechist described her as a blank slate, could know that the Virgin Mary had been born without sin. Pope Pius IX had proclaimed the dogma of the Immaculate Conception only four years earlier. This was the belief that the Blessed Mother was preserved from original sin and had never sinned.

Father Peyramale asked Bernadette, what those words meant to her. Bernadette shook her head. The words that she had so carefully repeated held no meaning for her. The priest looked quietly at the child and then sharply dismissed her. Closing the door behind her, he wept. The rosebush had not bloomed in the grotto on the Feast of the Annunciation, but a sense of wonder and gratitude had taken root in the priest. The Virgin Mary, he marveled, had visited Bernadette Soubirous, daughter of Lourdes and child of the *cachot*.

The Mother of God beckoned Bernadette two more times. On the morning of Easter Tuesday, April 7, Bernadette prayed at the grotto in the early morning. While in ecstasy, she did not feel the flame of a candle licking at her hand, and later she showed no sign of injury. "She still wants her chapel," Bernadette would say later about what Our Lady made known to her.[10]

Three more months passed before the Virgin and Bernadette met again. In the meantime Bernadette received her First Communion on June 3, the Feast of Corpus Christi.

On July 16, 1858, the Feast of Our Lady of Mount Carmel, Bernadette received once again the irresistible invitation to go to the grotto. The path to it, at the order of the authorities, had been blocked to keep the crowds out. Disguised by an oversized cloak and accompanied by her young aunt, Lucile Castérot, and two other girls, Bernadette ran to the meadow that faced the rocks of

Massabielle but did not cross the River Gave. The girls knelt among the other pilgrims who were there praying as the sun set.

"It seemed to me that I was at the Grotto, at the same distance as the other times," Bernadette recalled. "I had never seen her so beautiful."[11] It was the final rendezvous, the last time that Bernadette Soubirous would ever see the beautiful lady, the Immaculate Conception.

Bishop Bertrand Sévère Laurence, the bishop of Tarbes, set in motion a canonical commission of inquiry following the last apparition. He charged its twelve members with investigating the events of the grotto, including testimony from Bernadette. On January 18, 1862, in the name of the Church, Bishop Laurence issued a letter declaring, "We judge: that Mary Immaculate, the Mother of God, really did appear to Bernadette Soubirous, on eighteen occasions from 11th February 1858 at the Grotto of Massabielle, near the town of Lourdes; that these Apparitions bear the characteristics of truth; that the faithful can believe them as true."[12]

Following the apparitions, Bernadette attended the hospice school founded by the Sisters of Charity of Nevers as a day pupil (1858–1860) and then as a "destitute boarder" (1860–1866), a position Father Peyramale suggested in order to shield her from the crowds who wanted to see and touch the girl who had glimpsed heaven. Drawn to the religious life, Bernadette asked to join the Sisters of Charity.

At the request of Bishop Laurence, Bernadette delayed entering the community until after the first Lourdes chapel, the Crypt, was opened. At that time she marched in the procession at the grotto, fulfilling Our Lady's request. On July 4, 1866, Bernadette Soubirous boarded a train that would take her nearly 500 miles from Lourdes, to the sisters' motherhouse in Nevers. She would never see the grotto or her family again.

chapter two

. • . .

MIRACLES, CURES AND BLESSINGS

PERHAPS ONE OF THE GREATEST MIRACLES OF THE GROTTO OF Massabielle is that none were ever promised yet thousands have been attributed to the intercession of Our Lady of Lourdes. Of the some seven thousand cures reviewed by the Medical Bureau of Lourdes, the Church has declared sixty-seven to be miracles.

From Catherine Latapie-Chouat, the first *miraculée*, whose injured fingers regained movement, to Anna Santaniello, whose miraculous recovery from a heart condition was made public in 2005, we can trace a history of God's healing grace.[1]

Bishop Laurence authenticated the first roll call of cured individuals, all healed in 1858, when he proclaimed the apparitions of the Blessed Virgin true in his mandate of January 18, 1862. The cures of all seven individuals—three women, one man, two teenagers and one toddler—were attributed to bathing in or applying the water from the spring of Massabielle.

The bishop had earlier directed his commission investigating the apparitions to leave no stone unturned. He urged the priests to meet not only with the doctors who cared for the sick before their cures but also with scientists specializing in geology, physics and chemistry. No rational explanations for the cures came forth. "Science, which was consulted on this subject, responded negatively," Bishop Laurence said. "These cures are thus the work of God."[2]

- Catherine Latapie-Chouat, thirty-eight, suffered paralysis in her fingers when a tree fell on her hand. She prayed at the grotto and then bathed her arm in the waters. Immediately she was able to stretch and bend her fingers. Later that day she gave birth to her third child, who eventually became a priest.

- Louis Bouriette, fifty-four, a quarryman, had lost complete vision in his right eye during a mine explosion. He asked "Our Lady of the Grotto" to be with him as he bathed his eye several times with water from the spring. His sight was totally restored.

- Doctors had told Blaisette Cazenave, fifty, that her eye infections were incurable. In imitation of Bernadette, she drank from the spring and washed her face there. She did so again, and her eyelid sores vanished, as did the pain and inflammation.

- Henri Busquet was only sixteen when he begged his parents to take him from his hometown of Nay to Lourdes. His suffering from a sudden onset of tuberculosis had become unbearable. A neighbor gave the teenager Lourdes water. After praying with his family, Henri applied a bandage soaked in the Lourdes water to the abscessed tumor on his neck. Within two days the tuberculin ulcer had healed and the infection was gone.

- The story of two-year-old Justin Bouhort has been made famous by the movie *The Song of Bernadette,* based on the book of the same name by Franz Werfel.[3] The toddler was very small and could not walk. Various illnesses had weakened him to the point of death.

His mother took him to the grotto and prayed. Then she plunged the baby into the cold waters of the spring, ignoring bystanders' protests. The next day a rosy-cheeked Justin walked for the first time. On December 8, 1933, at the age of seventy-seven, Justin attended the canonization ceremonies of Bernadette.

- Bedridden for more than twenty years and paralyzed on her left side, Madeleine Rizan, fifty-eight, believed she had reached life's end. On taking a few sips of Lourdes water offered by her daughter, who also applied it to her face and body, Madeleine instantly recovered.

- After reading about the cure of Madeleine Rizan in the newspaper, the father of Marie Moreau obtained water from Lourdes. An infection had robbed Marie, nearly seventeen, of most of her eyesight. The family began praying a novena, and Marie placed a compress soaked with Lourdes water to her eyes. The next morning when she removed it, her vision had been restored.

These "works of God" during the year of the apparitions were just the start. Each year increasing numbers of pilgrims shared their stories of healing. It was not until the early twentieth century, however, that the Church recognized the next round of miraculous cures.

In 1905 Pope Pius X called for a screening process to evaluate the claimed cures of Lourdes. The Medical Bureau of Lourdes assumed this responsibility.

Located on the second floor of the Accueil John Paul II, the Medical Bureau is to this day the first point of contact for a pilgrim who believes he or she has been healed. It is here that the pilgrim comes for examination. If the head of the Medical Bureau judges that the claim has substance, he invites doctors registered with the bureau and present in the shrine that day—of any faith or nationality—to attend the consultation. If there is agreement that there appears to be a cure, the pilgrim must return to meet with the Medical Bureau over several years.

In the eighteenth century Cardinal Lambertini, the future Pope Benedict XIV, established the stringent criteria against which a cure is measured. Specifically, the illness or condition healed must be serious and incurable, the healing must be sudden and without relapse, and no medical treatment must be given.

The dossiers of promising healings are passed on to the International Medical Committee of Lourdes, formed in 1947 and comprised of specialists from all over the world. These experts evaluate the results of the repeated physical and psychological examinations, medical case notes, laboratory records and accounts of medical and other witnesses in light of current medicine and science. The bishop of Tarbes and Lourdes cochairs the committee with a physician nominated by him. A vote of the members determines whether a cure is inexplicable according to present scientific knowledge.

If a majority reaches a positive decision, the committee then forwards the file to the bishop of the diocese of the person who has been cured. The local bishop empanels a medical committee to consider the findings. Based on the committee's recommendations, he then decides in favor of a miracle or abstains from declaring the cure to be miraculous in nature.

Using this framework in reviewing past and current claims, one of the first cures recognized as miraculous in 1908 was exceptional in nearly all aspects. A fallen tree had crushed the left leg of Pierre de Rudder, fifty-two years of age. Infection had set in quickly, preventing the compound fracture from healing. For eight years Pierre hobbled on crutches in pain, unfit for labor and facing the amputation of his leg.

In desperation Pierre made a pilgrimage to the Belgian town of Oostacker, where there is a small replica of the Lourdes grotto. Within minutes of praying to the Blessed Virgin for assistance, Pierre's bones knit back together. He was able to walk without crutches, and he lived an active life for twenty-three more years. His body was exhumed in a later inquiry, and an examination of his leg showed the break and healing. Pierre's was one of some sixty cures the Medical Bureau has declared miraculous using the Lambertini criteria.

Vittorio Micheli of Italy numbers among the most recent *miraculés*. In 1963 twenty-three-year-old Vittorio, suffering from a cancerous tumor, was lowered into the baths on a stretcher. Follow-up tests revealed his reconstructed hipbone with no tumor. Pain-free, Vittorio resumed walking as well as living life to the fullest.

A blocked carotid artery causing paralysis, blackouts and vision problems had diminished Serge Perrin, forty-one, a native of France. In May 1970, at the anointing of the sick at Lourdes, Serge felt a wave of change. His doctors later confirmed that he had been cured.

Delizia Cirolli was only twelve years old when physicians advised her parents that the tumor swelling her knee was incurable and potentially fatal. They advised amputation, a plan of treatment that her parents rejected. Delizia's friends and family raised enough money to send her from Sicily to Lourdes during the summer of 1976. She returned unchanged. As her condition worsened near Christmas, many prayed to Our Lady of Lourdes for her total recovery, which is exactly what came about.

A nurse at a French hospital, Jean-Pierre Bely understood well what the diagnosis of multiple sclerosis he received in 1972 meant for his future. In 1987, bedridden and "100 percent disabled," Jean-Pierre made a pilgrimage to Lourdes. After the anointing of the sick, he experienced an overwhelming sense of peace. Then he realized that he had regained his sense of touch and his mobility.

Anna Santaniello of Italy, the final beneficiary of a recognized cure as of this writing, suffered severe heart disease following rheumatic fever. Labored breathing made it difficult for her to speak and to walk. The lack of oxygen gave her face and lips a bluish cast. In 1952, at the age of forty-one, she was taken to the baths on a stretcher. She left on her own and walked in the candlelight procession that night. The doctors who examined her found her to be in good health, having a regular pulse and heart rhythm and breathing without restrictions. She worked for many years as a pediatric nurse before retiring.

Of the sixty-seven miraculous cures recorded to date, some commonalities emerge.[4] Most of the *miraculés* have been women (fifty-four), and most, not unexpectedly, have been French (fifty-five). All were born in Europe. At the time of being cured, they ranged in age from two to sixty-four years old, about half of them thirty years old and younger.

Tuberculosis, a common disease during the nineteenth and early twentieth centuries, was the condition reported most often. From 1950 until today, four individuals with multiple sclerosis have been completely cured. Cancer, heart disease, infections, blindness and injuries caused by accidents are just some of the other conditions of which *miraculés* have been healed.

While the demographics provide a snapshot of the men, women, teens and children whose health was inexplicably restored, how they were cured sheds additional light. For a majority of the *miraculés* (forty-nine of sixty-seven), the water from the spring of Massabielle was instrumental. Most had bathed in the water (thirty-nine), and a smaller number had either applied (eight) or drunk it (two). Eleven traced their recovery to the Eucharist; these received a Eucharistic blessing (eight) or Communion (three). Some were healed after receiving the anointing of the sick, praying at the shrine or returning from a pilgrimage. Six individuals who received healing, including Pierre de Rudder, whose leg was made whole, were cured without ever visiting Lourdes.

Among the miraculous cures the Church has recognized, only four have been designated since 1975. Bishop Jacques Perrier, bishop of Tarbes and Lourdes, has raised this as an issue. He does not question whether spontaneous cures happen—dozens are authenticated each year at Lourdes—but whether it's possible against today's medical landscape to validate a cure as a miracle. Of particular concern is the requirement that the person cured has not taken medicine or, if he or she has, that the medicine or treatment was ineffective.

When Cardinal Lambertini developed the criteria for recognizing a healing as miraculous, medical knowledge was limited. The discovery that lemons prevent scurvy is the one advance during his lifetime (1675–1758) that survives in medical history timelines. Diagnostic equipment was rare; the stethoscope had not even been invented. X-rays would be introduced more than 100 years after Lambertini's death, as would the common painkiller aspirin. Given the dearth of medication and therapies, it was not difficult during Lambertini's time to isolate the exclusive cause for a cure. Similarly, at the time of the apparitions during the nineteenth century, many of the sick who came to Lourdes did so simply because they had no medical recourse.

In an editorial published in the diocesan *Bulletin Religieux* and later reprinted in *Lourdes Magazine,* Bishop Perrier noted that enforcing the Lambertini requirement that medicine should play no role in a healing is challenging. "This renders impossible, for example, the recognition of any miraculous cure of cancer," wrote Bishop Perrier. Once cancer is detected, he explained, a responsible physician immediately and prudently starts a plan of treatment for his or her patient. "This person comes to Lourdes and regains his health at a precise moment which he will remember until he dies, in his body as much as in his mind. This healing is complete and stable." However, the healing described would never be acknowledged as miraculous because prior and effective medical treatment was given. While recognizing that a miracle in the canonical sense is always possible, the bishop questioned whether an approach that is more respectful of both the person and faith should not be considered.[5]

A press conference in March 2006 in Paris featured a paper prepared by Professor François-Bernard Michel, cochair of the International Medical Committee of Lourdes. He described a new three-staged initiative for recognizing healings at Lourdes:

1. At the first stage the officer of the Medical Bureau thoroughly evaluates a person who believes he or she has received the grace of a spontaneous or extraordinary cure. If the "declared cure" passes inspection, it is classified as an "unexpected cure."
2. The second stage involves critical examination of medical documents before and after the "unexpected cure," looking for evidence supporting an indisputable change from a known illness or condi-

tion to restored health. Additionally, the cure must show signs of being completely out of character with the development of the illness. If these requirements are met, the "unexpected cure" becomes a "confirmed cure."

3. During the third and final stage, the International Medical Committee affirms the "exceptional character" of the cure relative to present scientific knowledge. The bishop of Tarbes and Lourdes then forwards the file for further review to the diocese where the person who was cured lives.

The number of cures and miracles the Church affirms will always seem few in comparison to the millions of pilgrims who journey to Lourdes, as they do not include the blessings that countless numbers receive. These graces, not recognized by scientific inquiry, renew both body and soul. God blesses many pilgrims by way of the unexpected—perhaps an acceptance of one's health or loss, a lightening of a burden, an easing of physical, emotional or psychological pain or even the gift of new life.

Elizabeth Grinder, who directs the U.S. National Rosary Pilgrimage, travels in the company of many pilgrims who are sick or have special needs. Most will return to the United States with the same health problems with which they arrived. Many will, however, be changed in spirit and outlook.

"It's humbling to be a part of this pilgrimage. The first year that I went, I almost felt guilty," says Liz. "I was on such an adrenaline high in witnessing the transformation of people. I truly believe that no one leaves Lourdes without something."

Liz credits the changed hearts to Mary's love, which encourages pilgrims. "The more I go, the more I realize how embraced we are by the Blessed Mother. You really witness humanity at its absolute best," she believes. "I often say Lourdes is somewhere suspended between heaven and earth, because nowhere else on earth can you see the compassion and the joy in situations where you would not expect it." While people might not be physically healed, she believes they become better equipped to accept their own uniqueness.

Father Joseph Allen, O.P., the spiritual director for the same pilgrimage, agrees. Father Allen is currently provincial director of his Dominican community's missions in Africa, the Solomon Islands, the Philippines and Pakistan. Over the years he has served as pastor, prior and administrator of the order's seminary and shrines.

"I think everybody comes home a new person," Father Allen says. "They may not have gotten the specific cure that they were looking for, but most people come back renewed in the spirit and renewed in their conviction of their faith."

That is exactly what happened to Sandy and Jack Crotty. Twenty-three years ago an accident at Jack's workplace seriously disabled him. In that instant Sandy Crotty stepped beyond being wife and mother of four into the uncharted territory of caregiver. "No one knows what that entails," Sandy says.

The Federal Association of the Order of Malta invited Jack and Sandy to be their guests on their international pilgrimage to Lourdes. "Life altering" is how Sandy sums up the experience. "When you're standing and kneeling on the ground where Mary appeared to this little French girl, something comes over you," she says. "You know the Blessed Mother is there, and she's going to help you."

For Sandy and Jack that help came in the persons of the Knights and Dames of Malta. "The way those people care in their hearts," Sandy says, "is incredible." Not only did they anticipate every need

Jack had, but they also recognized Sandy for her skill and devotion in caring for her husband. Back home in Syracuse, Sandy says that Jack's health has improved somewhat. However, the long-lasting blessing of Lourdes, she believes, is the grace they received to accept what is. "I know now that it's going to be OK," says Sandy.

Bill Olson, a deacon by vocation and a lawyer by profession, makes himself available—both in his home diocese of Davenport, Iowa, and at Lourdes—to those who need someone to listen. Deacon Bill believes God gives the grace to many who come to Lourdes to face what is difficult in their lives. For too long, he says, many have numbed the pain of the invisible wounds of the heart—often the aftershocks of loss, trauma or abuse.

"Many people tell me why they have to come to Lourdes, and invariably it's connected with a hidden injury," Deacon Bill says. Healing at Lourdes takes place, he believes, in going to confession, drinking or bathing in the waters, meditating before the Blessed Sacrament on Christ's sacrifice and joining one's own pain with his sufferings.

Jamie Jensen left Lourdes not cured but in many ways new. Jamie, who is in his twenties, has spastic cerebral palsy, a condition in which too much muscle tone results in stiff muscles and exaggerated movements. As Jamie explains it, when someone with spastic CP meets cold water, the outcome is usually more spasms. When Jamie went into the baths, his body relaxed, and he remained less spastic for more than a day. But the real "lift" came, Jamie says, after he returned home and realized all that he had accomplished physically and spiritually during his pilgrimage.

Kevin White, K.M., a Knight of the Western Association of the Order of Malta, recalls the grace of acceptance that one family received. "We had the privilege of bringing an eight-year-old boy and his family with us to Lourdes," Kevin says. Shortly after their return the young boy passed away. "At the funeral his father put his arms around me. He said, 'We will never forget the Lourdes experience, because it helped us prepare for this day, and it helped us to accept God's will.'"

"I'm living on grace," Sister Maria-Paulina Sterling says cheerfully of the blessings she has received since returning from Lourdes. Sister Maria-Paulina, who uses a cane to walk and a wheelchair for long distances, went to the shrine with the North American Lourdes Volunteers. "To make a long story short," she says, "I had exhausted all medical avenues. My doctor said I needed a miracle and suggested my going to Lourdes."

Sister Maria-Paulina had been diagnosed after entering religious life with three related diseases: multiple sclerosis, ankylosing spondylitis and pyoderma gangrenosum. Within a week of making her final vows, her health took a sharp turn for the worse. She was hospitalized repeatedly.

"I was losing the use of my voice, because my lungs would not inflate enough to give me the breath and vocal support needed to produce sung sound," Sister Maria-Paulina recalls. This could traumatize anyone, but especially Sister Maria-Paulina, who as a church musician plays the organ and sings.

Now "people are saying, 'Your voice is back,'" Sister Maria-Paulina reports of the steady improvement that she too has noticed. Her walking—always difficult because of the multiple sclerosis—has also improved.

Beyond her physical gains, Sister shares what she considers an even greater blessing: She and another sister are forming a new religious community in the archdiocese of Chicago. "The Sisters of the Real Presence of Our Lord Jesus Christ is a monastic/active community whose charism is to pray for the spiritual intentions and temporal needs of all priests in front of our Lord Jesus in the Blessed Sacrament," Sister Maria-Paulina says. The sisters will take a fourth vow, to promote and defend the truths of the Catholic faith, in addition to the three traditional vows of poverty, chastity and obedience. "I'm so grateful," Sister Maria-Paulina says, "because I know in my heart that all these spiritual fruits are a result of my pilgrimage to Lourdes."

Jim Miller also credits Lourdes with changing his life. Serving in the Air Force in Germany during the late 1950s, Jim slipped off the wing of a bomber on which he was working. The damage to his foot—a torn metatarsal arch and broken toes—was so severe that osteoarthritis immediately set in. Jim spent the next twelve months hospitalized, first in Germany and then Stateside in Walter Reed Hospital. Physicians doubted that he would walk again. Fortunately he did, but never without pain and never without special support shoes.

After bathing in the waters of the spring of Massabielle in 2004, Jim sensed a change. "There was no pain, but I thought it was because of the cold water," he recalls. The intense pain he suffered for many years has never returned.

When Karl and Katie Orbon went to Lourdes, they prayed that God would bless them with a child. Katie had recently had surgery, and she had learned that her health might be at risk if she were to become pregnant. The Orbons placed their desire in the hands of the Blessed Mother. "We wanted to have children," Karl explains. "We just wanted to give that whole situation into her care to intercede."

Several months later Katie discovered she was pregnant. On April 9, 2007, Maximilian Joseph Orbon arrived. Katie's anticipated health problem never materialized. Holding baby Max in his arms, Karl laughs and says, "Not a certifiable miracle, but our miracle."

Patricia Coghlan has never gone to Lourdes, but she has a similar story, which she has delighted in sharing over the years with her children and grandchildren. "My mother-in-law went to Lourdes. She prayed for a miracle," Patty begins and then adds, "I married him."

Elizabeth Sheedy married William Madden Coghlan in 1916. The couple was blessed two years later with a daughter, Marcella. When Elizabeth could not become pregnant again, she took action. Traveling from the United States to her native Ireland, she then made her way to Lourdes and petitioned the Blessed Mother. On Mother's Day the following year, William Patrick Coghlan, Patty's future husband, was born.

Father Clinton Zadroga believes that these many blessings—while not miracles or cures in the purest sense—are encouragements from God to persevere. Father Clint experienced a healing of his own from Temporomandibular Joint (TMJ) disorder, which involves severe pain in the jaw, after splashing Lourdes water on his face.

"I think of the Transfiguration. Peter, James and John went up the mountain. Jesus gave them an amazing experience—a glimpse of his glory. He wanted that experience to carry them through the difficulties ahead," says Father Clint, a priest of the diocese of Pittsburgh and a convert to the faith. "Lourdes does that for us."

The blessings of Lourdes go deeper yet. When a paralyzed man on a stretcher was brought to Jesus for healing, our Lord immediately said to him, "Take heart, my son; your sins are forgiven." When pressed by the crowd, who questioned his authority, Jesus asked,

"Which is easier, to say, 'Your sins are forgiven,' or to say, 'Rise and walk'?" Jesus commanded the paralytic to "rise, take up your bed and go home" (Matthew 9:2, 5, 6). Jesus clearly gave priority to the conversion of the soul, the very same priority echoed in the message of Lourdes.

So does Dr. Michael Martinelli. The cardiologist from Albany, New York, serves as the volunteer medical director for North American Lourdes Volunteers. "As physicians we are blessed with the opportunity not just to address the physical needs of our patients but to truly bring to them the message of our Lord's spiritual healing. This is the message of Lourdes," he says. "This is the message that Our Lady wishes to convey to her children."

It is through the miraculous physical cures that occur at Lourdes, Dr. Martinelli believes, that many are able to accept the invitation to participate in an even deeper and more profound transformation of the spirit. "The physical cure, while important," Dr. Martinelli says, "pales in comparison to a spiritual cure, which is infinite. It is the spiritual cure that saves us for eternity."

Father Dominic Mary Garner, M.F.V.A., welcomes pilgrims to the Shrine of the Most Blessed Sacrament at Our Lady of the Angels Monastery in Hanceville, Alabama. He celebrates Mass for the pilgrims and the Poor Clare Nuns and also hears confessions at the shrine. As a pilgrim to Lourdes, Father Dominic has observed healings of moral, spiritual, emotional and psychological wounds— wounds that, he says, can be far worse than physical suffering.

"Not only is the grace available from God through the hands of Our Lady and the intercession of Saint Bernadette, but at Lourdes people suffering from these nonphysical difficulties and problems witness the message of Our Lady of Lourdes in action," he says.

They see firsthand the Lourdes volunteers living the gospel by performing, at no personal worldly gain, acts of sacrifice and charity. They encounter the sick and handicapped who have united their sufferings to Christ. Father Dominic believes that, as a result, Lourdes becomes the seedbed for conversion of the heart, interior healings and turning away from sin.

"Many are reconciled with God and...go to confession," he says. "We've had many people convert within days from a life of sin to a complete, deep, long-lasting conversion. Part of it is the witness of seeing sacrifice and charity in action and, more fundamentally, the work of grace."

It is these spiritual "cures" that Bishop Laurence recognized nearly 150 years ago in addition to the physical cures. According to Bishop Laurence, it is through these "wonders of grace" of Lourdes that Christian souls are strengthened in virtue, indifferent souls return to the faith, and obstinate souls reconcile with God. These graces, "which have a universal and lasting character, can only have God as their author," Bishop Laurence proclaimed in recognizing the apparitions.[6] The Lourdes we know today is built upon this.

chapter three

.   •   .

DRAWN BY FAITH OR CURIOSITY, PEOPLE FROM ALL PARTS OF the world go on pilgrimage to Lourdes, the most visited Marian shrine in Europe. When all is said and done, many pilgrims will measure their experience not by how far they travel but by how close they come to God.

Cardinal Joseph Ratzinger, now Pope Benedict XVI, urged Catholics in a Holy Thursday homily to remember their purpose in life: "We are only guests on earth; we are pilgrims in the profoundest sense, that the earth is not ultimate, and we are on our way to the new world."[1] Tucking this insight in with the luggage might help men, women and children embarking for Lourdes to view their pilgrimage within this larger frame.

Sister Anne Marie Gill, T.O.R., who frequently accompanies groups to Lourdes, reminds us, "Our whole life is a pilgrimage. We go on little pilgrimages--miniature versions of our life pilgrimage--seeking God. As much as we feel we have our feet planted here, pilgrimages remind us that our goal is to end up in heaven for all eternity with God." The pilgrim's road to Lourdes converges with the road of faith, leading to our final destination, our eternal home.

Pilgrimages have always played an important part in Church life and have been recognized as a gift of grace. In celebrating their faith, Christians have journeyed to places where the memory of Christ is present, the history of the Church is recalled or the Blessed Mother and saints are revered.[2]

Christian pilgrimages to the Holy Land can be traced back to the apostolic age. The glory days of pilgrimage, however, surfaced much later, in the Middle Ages. Men and women, priests and laity, royalty and commoners left behind the comforts of home to travel arduous roads to a shrine or sacred place. They set their sights most often on the Holy Land, the shrines of Saints Peter and Paul in Rome and the Cathedral of Santiago de Compostela in Spain, where the remains of the apostle Saint James the Great are said to be buried. For those who could not travel long distances, pilgrimages to the tombs of saints of local repute—including, for example, Saint Martin of Tours, Saint Thomas Beckett of Canterbury and Saint Francis of Assisi—nicely sufficed.

Before setting out for the more remote shrines, pilgrims of the Middle Ages donned the clothes of a penitent, a long gray robe and a broad-brimmed hat. These clothes would be recognized as those of pilgrims throughout the lands they would cross. They each shouldered a pouch for carrying necessities, placed a staff in hand and carried the written authorization of the local bishop or abbot.

On the way pilgrims would be grateful for the blessing they had received before leaving, as they would encounter hardships of every stripe, including poor sanitation, extremes of cold and heat, disease, attacks by highwaymen on the roads, pirates on the seas and swindlers, who marked them as easy prey. So great were the risks that several religious orders and confraternities dedicated themselves to protecting and assisting the pilgrims. And the pilgrims, motivated by their desire to do penance, seek a blessing or offer thanks to God, continued on their way despite the obstacles. They seldom made the journey alone but, for added safety and unity, shared the companionship of pilgrimage.

Centuries later companionship also characterized the visits of Bernadette to the Grotto of Massabielle. From the first to the last apparition, she never ventured there alone. The initial company of her sister and a friend grew to include her schoolmates, family, neighbors and countless others unknown to her. Many came not only to watch Bernadette in ecstasy but also to pray along with her. Near the end of the apparitions, at least eight thousand people— twice the population of Lourdes—crowded the area surrounding the grotto and witnessed Bernadette with her eyes fixed on the niche in the rock.

With the Church's recognition of the apparitions as authentic in 1862 and the inauguration of the railway to Lourdes in 1866, the circle of pilgrims expanded from parishes in the immediate countryside to dioceses throughout France and eventually to points all over Europe. Travelers from other continents soon joined the steady stream of visitors to Lourdes. About two decades following Our Lady's appearances to Bernadette, the first pilgrims from America crossed the Atlantic by ocean liner and then traveled overland to the grotto.

Air transportation opened the doors to many more pilgrims during the twentieth century. By today's standards, however, the early flights from North America required both patience and perseverance.

Writing his bishop from Lourdes on July 14, 1947, Father James R. Cox described the first charter air pilgrimage from the United

States, a TWA flight accommodating thirty-two pilgrims. "Our pilgrimage to Lourdes by air, the first in history, was very interesting," he wrote on stationery imprinted with *Grand Hotel Moderne—Soubirous Frères*. "We left Pittsburgh Monday, July 7, at 4 PM and were in Paris the next day at 7:30 PM, with stops at New York, Gander [Newfoundland], Eire [Ireland], and Paris."[3] The total air time, Father Cox estimated, was seventeen hours. Once in Paris, the pilgrims boarded a train for Lourdes.

Father Cox's devotion to Our Lady of Lourdes preceded his reputation as "the pastor of the poor" who led twenty-five thousand unemployed workers to Washington, D.C., during the Depression. As a youth his failing eyesight had stood between him and his dream of becoming a priest. After physicians who had treated his eyes for three years despaired, the young Cox turned to the Blessed Mother.

"All hope of cure was abandoned by everybody except myself," he later recalled, "and I knew Our Lady would help me. Lourdes water was procured and used." Two hours later his eyes were cured.[4] In gratitude for this miracle, Father Cox celebrated Mass at Lourdes while serving as a chaplain with American Expeditionary Forces during World War I. He escorted twenty pilgrimages there before his death in 1951.

Chartered planes began flying pilgrims directly to Lourdes in 1948 with the opening of Tarbes Airport. These groups often carried the sick on stretchers.

In 1954 the U.S. National Rosary Pilgrimage sponsored its first national pilgrimage to Lourdes. Elizabeth Grinder, the daughter of the late John Hodgson, the founder of this contingent, serves as executive director of the pilgrimage, which continues to this day.

Much like the pilgrims who set out in the Middle Ages, people from every rank and social status have found their way to Lourdes. Within the first fifty years of the apparitions, the king of Portugal (1878), the prince of Wales and future king of England (1879), the empress of Brazil (1887), the queen of Serbia (1902) and the king of Spain (1905) came to the grotto.[5] Six pilgrims who would later be pope visited: Monsignor Della Chiesa (Benedict XV), Cardinal Ratti (Pius XI), Cardinal Pacelli (Pius XII), Cardinal Roncalli (John XXIII), Cardinal Montini (Paul VI), Cardinal Luciani (John Paul I) and Cardinal Wojtla (John Paul II). The latter visited Lourdes five times during his life—first as a parish priest, then as archbishop, later as cardinal of Krakow and finally, in 1983 and 2004, as the reigning pope, the first pontiff to do so.[6] Pope Benedict XVI is expected to visit Lourdes during its 150th jubilee.

The majority of visitors today are surprisingly not members of any particular pilgrimage group or organization. They come, perhaps with friends or family, and simply enter the gates of the Sanctuary of Our Lady of Lourdes, as the shrine is known. Lourdes offers a program to these "day pilgrims" or "passing pilgrims," who may be visiting for just a short time. During the peak season (July through September), the Sanctuary invites them to gather in the morning (currently 8:30 AM) at the Statue of the Crowned Virgin. Guides from the Daily Pilgrimage Service—usually priests or seminarians—invite them to sample a few of the spiritual riches Lourdes has to offer. They attend Mass together in the Sanctuary, hear the story of Lourdes, make the Stations of the Cross and process together behind the banner "Day Pilgrims" for the Eucharistic and candlelight processions.

The diocesan, national and international pilgrimages typically range in size from groups of about 100 to tens of thousands, including people with and without disabilities. Each pilgrimage organization registers with the Sanctuary. Each has at its center something in common, perhaps geography (for example, the French National Pilgrimage, Dublin Diocesan Pilgrimage and UNITALSI of Italy), a shared spirituality (for example, Order of Malta, Montfortians, Carmelites, Franciscans), a particular life-stage (for example, Teams of Our Lady, consisting of married couples and the Frat de Lourdes, a youth pilgrimage) or a given heritage (for example, Pilgrimage of Gypsies and Traveling People). Each typically has an identifying banner, behind which the pilgrims march in the Eucharistic and candlelight Marian processions, and possibly a piece of clothing that identifies them as members of the pilgrimage.

The Dublin Diocesan Pilgrimage provides an example of the workings of a pilgrimage organization. Since 1949 people of the diocese have traveled to Lourdes each fall, the only exception being a year in which there was a general workers' strike in France. Led by their cardinal or archbishop, about 2,000 people make up a pilgrimage cohort, including approximately 175 individuals who are sick; 500 doctors, nurses, chaplains and volunteers; and an additional group of 200 young adults from the secondary schools and colleges, called the Dublin Diocesan Hospitalité, who care for the spiritual, medical and everyday needs of the sick pilgrims. Individual pilgrims from the different parishes of the diocese round out the annual pilgrimage.[7]

Smaller groups—organized perhaps by a parish, a club, an association or a travel agency—also register with the Sanctuary of Our Lady of Lourdes. Chaplains accompanying the pilgrimage groups may reserve one or more of the many churches for Mass.

Pope John Paul II captured concisely why so many pilgrims have visited and will continue to visit this small town in the Pyrénées. "When the Virgin Mary appeared to Bernadette in the grotto at Massabielle, she began a dialogue between *Heaven and earth* which has lasted through time and continues to this day," the pope said on the eve of the Assumption in 1983. "Speaking to the young girl, Mary asked that people should come here *in procession,* as if to signify that this dialogue cannot be limited to words, but must become *a journey at her side along the pilgrim way of faith, hope, and love.*"[8]

In journeying alongside Our Lady, many pilgrims of the third millennium choose to step out of an increasingly secular world for a time and take stock of their true destination in life. This departure—both figuratively and literally—allows the pilgrim to repair spiritually.

"Because our culture is so overwhelmingly secular—without our even realizing it—there is a certain malaise that comes," suggests Father Clinton Zadroga. "One symptom is the gradual changing of priorities. It's sad to say, but faith, family and relationships are not the priorities of a secularized culture." In such a culture, Father Clint believes, we lose our sense of God and others and turn inward.

"A pilgrimage is a way of stepping out of that and having your faith renewed. A pilgrimage is like a retreat on the move. With a retreat or pilgrimage, you get a true sense of what's important—a fresh, broader perspective," he adds.

Cora Sullivan, a first-time pilgrim to Lourdes, would agree. Living in an age in which status matters more than faith, she says, robs believers of what is important and true. "I think life has become burdensome. We have taken that upon ourselves," she says. "We think we need more, but we don't."

Cora regards a pilgrimage to Lourdes as a way to renew her faith. In addition, undertaking a pilgrimage to Lourdes fulfills a promise Cora, an American, made to herself as a young girl growing up in Northern Ireland. Having chosen Bernadette as her patron for confirmation, she dreamed of visiting Lourdes. "It never left my mind. It's one of the things that I wanted to do in my lifetime," Cora recalled before departing for France. "This is the moment."

A personal connection has inspired many a pilgrim to visit Lourdes. Thomas Joyce is a software engineer at a major university who has completed studies in spiritual and ministerial formation. He made the pilgrimage to Lourdes with his sister Beth in thanksgiving for the health of their mother.

"My mother is named after Saint Bernadette, and I've always had a fascination with Lourdes," he notes. Some years ago it appeared that their mother had a progressive type of illness. As it turned out, Mrs. Joyce is one of a small percentage of people whose blood profile indicates the condition while it is not present. Before knowing that his mother was absolutely healthy, however, Tom stormed the heavens.

"I prayed to Our Lady of Lourdes and Saint Bernadette for intercession." Going on pilgrimage, he said, expressed his thanks to both and, in a special way, recognized the thread connecting his mother to the saint and to Our Lady and ultimately to him.

This was not, however, the only reason that Tom signed on. "There isn't a Christian alive—a Catholic alive—who, if they were completely honest, wouldn't admit at some level a need to go spiritually deeper," he says. In going to Lourdes, Tom says, the pilgrim encounters the Mother of God, who points us to her Son. "In our own lives, our hearts need to be strengthened and our souls need to be strengthened," he says. A pilgrimage, with its time away from life's distractions, allows for that. On pilgrimage Tom finds "face time" with God, a time in which all else fades and what remains is God and he alone. "Yes, I went for personal reasons for my mom, but I also went because I just decided that I needed this too," Tom concludes.

The itinerary of a pilgrimage, as Tom Joyce suggests, takes one deeper interiorly. Louise Sutton, who along with her son-in-law joined pilgrims traveling to Lourdes from Roanoke, Virginia, speaks of the spiritual road map that guided her. The spiritual director, a priest, encouraged Louise and her fellow pilgrims to consider why they were there, what their goal was and where they were going.

"We were reminded that this was not just a tour but a pilgrimage," says the retired director of a state child care office. "Everyone was tuned in to the real purpose. In all of this the Spirit of God was present."

Kathleen Gallagher, who works with troubled youth, has been in Lourdes four times. She says that each occasion has allowed her to go deeper in her faith. "When you set out with the heart of a pilgrim, you're not leaving any space between you and God," the wife, mother and lay Carmelite says. "You are open to being touched however God chooses to touch you."

Father Régis-Marie de La Teyssonnière, a priest of the archdiocese of Paris, is a Chaplain of Honor of Our Lady of Lourdes, a special distinction awarded to priests who most generously and enthusiastically serve the Sanctuary of Lourdes, accompanying or welcoming pilgrims. Fluent in five languages and a gifted writer and presenter, Father de La Teyssonnière, at the request of the bishop of Tarbes and Lourdes, has spoken across five continents about Mary's appearances at Lourdes, her message to Bernadette and the 150th anniversary of the apparitions. Father de La Teyssonnière suggests that pilgrims can discover in Bernadette the quintessential model for opening themselves to God at a deeper level.

"What a wonderful experience for Bernadette to see Our Lady, the Immaculate Conception, the Mother of God, eighteen times at the Lourdes Grotto! If we are thinking or reflecting about that, how can we not be touched by all it represents of beauty, happiness and wonderment?" Father de La Teyssonière asks. "But most important for this fourteen-year-old French girl," he believes, "was not the context but the content of each of her meetings with Mary. In fact, the eighteen apparitions are essentially a Christian life catechesis and a meeting with Jesus Christ."

According to Father de La Teyssonière, it was within the lessons of the grotto that the Blessed Virgin taught Bernadette the gospel, led her to her Son and gave her Christ the Savior. "I want to add that Mary's teaching is not a concept but an experience to enter," Father de La Teyssonnière says. The priest reminds pilgrims that the Blessed Virgin told Bernadette, "What I want to say to you doesn't need to be written."

The message of Lourdes for Bernadette and for today's pilgrims, he says, is a "message for the heart, understandable in a true relationship, a truly human experience." And, Father says, it is a message that is understandable for pilgrims who live, as Bernadette did, in a very concrete world. It is a world in which the poor, the sick and the weak are all too often marginalized.

The Blessed Virgin taught Bernadette, he explains, with what she could see, touch and experience. "Bernadette is invited to enter a grotto, to drink spring water, to wash from it and to carry the light," says Father de La Teyssonnière. "Rock, water and light are parts of the human experience, of the religious experience and of Christian revelation. Mary invites Bernadette to go further than the human level, to go further than the religious level, to reach the level of Christian revelation."

These basic elements of life—rock, water and light—become for Bernadette, Father de La Teyssonnière says, the place of meeting Jesus. This in turn prepares her to meet Jesus Christ in the sacraments of the Church. "Bernadette's experience is a pilgrimage led by Mary. She has to go out of her place, to walk, to go forward, to keep going. But at the same time this concrete pilgrimage is a pilgrimage deep in the heart," he says.

Karl Orbon, much like Father de La Teyssonnière, appreciates both the simplicity and physicality of the message of Lourdes for pilgrims. While holding advanced degrees in theology and philosophy, Karl believes that the world overcomplicates things when it comes to faith.

"Our Lady appeared to somebody who was a simple young girl," he says. The Blessed Virgin used that which was basic, empirical and sensible to introduce Bernadette and, by extension, pilgrims to something of greater spiritual value, Karl says. Christians should bring their bodies, minds and spirits to the pilgrimage, he says. "Walking, kneeling and doing these very earthbound things point us higher. There's a connection between this world and the next. What we do on this earth is connected to what is going on in heaven."

In traveling to Lourdes, many pilgrims discover that they are go-betweens. They bring to the Grotto of Massabielle the prayers and hopes of others. And they often bring back to those at home some remembrance to share, such as Lourdes water.

What surprises many pilgrims is not so much the requests from friends and family members for prayer but those from nodding acquaintances. In the past few years, Therese Brandl always has a story to tell about her travels. She has touched foot on every continent, including Antarctica. It was her pilgrimage trip to Lourdes, however, that prompted a bank teller converting her dollars to euros to ask a favor. "Pray for me," she said simply. Therese took seriously the teller's request. "Her name is Wendy," she said while waiting at the airport. "She's on my prayer list."

By the time Sister Maria-Paulina Sterling of Chicago arrived at Lourdes, she carried with her the petitions of several hundred individuals, most of whom she did not know. Sister went to Lourdes seeking a physical healing for herself but was anxious to carry the hopes of others with her. With the encouragement of her pastor, she placed a notice in the church bulletin inviting people to write out and give her their special prayer requests.

"People have faith," Sister Maria-Paulina says. "They knew that if I took their prayer intentions, they would be answered in God's way through the intercession of Our Lady of Lourdes."

To honor those petitions, Sister Maria-Paulina prayed the rosary at the grotto while she placed each petition—one by one—into the box designated for that purpose. "I had the responsibility to make sure I delivered them properly by praying to Our Lady, asking for her help," she says.

While clarifying that it was unnecessary to travel thousands of miles to Lourdes to pray for others, Karl Orbon acknowledges that it was a privilege to do so. "We looked at the grotto as a place we could come and bring spiritually all our family, friends and everybody we wanted to pray for," he says. "We wanted to bring everything before Our Lady and ask her, as our mother, to look after us."

At least one organization, the North American Lourdes Volunteers, encourages its pilgrims to take a person along in their hearts. By offering prayers, service and experiences at Lourdes, a volunteer shares the pilgrimage spiritually with another.

"That was, for me, one of the most fruitful things," Julie Wlotzko from Cincinnati says of her experience volunteering during her sophomore year at Franciscan University. "The Lord just placed someone on my heart to take with me." An early childhood education major, Julie hopes to enter the convent following her graduation.

According to Julie, Lourdes offers many tangible ways to remember others—living or dead: "You can take a bath for them, place their name in the grotto or light a candle for them."

Going to Lourdes on pilgrimage is not without its problems. For every peril and challenge the pilgrims of earlier ages faced, a counterpart can be found in the very real world of travel today. The expense, the time required, safety concerns, jet lag, lost luggage, language barriers, inadequate hotel rooms and the mix of personalities percolating on the pilgrim's way can all be off-putting. When several factors commingle, tensions arise. While these issues are part and parcel of international travel, they seem out of place on a Lourdes pilgrimage, with its quiet promise of renewal.

Tom Joyce speaks firsthand of practical problems he encountered. His luggage and that of about fifteen fellow pilgrims went missing twice during a ten-day pilgrimage. An international airline mistakenly set the luggage aside for seven days, returning it to the pilgrims just about when they were heading home. Once the group landed in the United States, the domestic airline failed to put their bags on board their connecting flight. Inconvenient, yes, Tom recalls, but not a tragedy by any means. Tom says that before leaving on a pilgrimage, it helps to prepare mentally for the unexpected.

Sister Anne Marie Gill, T.O.R., recommends adopting a realistic but faith-filled perspective. "On a pilgrimage, you're always going to have problems. Nothing is ever going to be perfect," she says. "Have a mindset that you're in God's providence, find his will in circumstances that evolve and make the best of it."

Nearly 700 years ago, Franciscan Friar Symon Simeonis, while en route to the Holy Land, suggested about the same. Anyone who undertakes a pilgrimage journey, he wrote in his diary, should carry along three sacks: "a sack of silver, a sack of patience, and a sack of faith."[9] When a problem arises, faith and patience will allow pilgrims to move beyond it and recognize the gift of Lourdes and one another.

Some Lourdes pilgrims find that traveling light enriches their experience. Kathleen Miller and her husband, Jim, both first-time pilgrims to Lourdes, limited the clothes they carried. They also substituted spiritual reading for the novels they typically slip into their carry-on bags for vacations. Pilgrims deliberately leave their worries and preoccupations behind, allowing them to focus on growing closer to God. "In removing ourselves of our baggage--the clothes or what concerns we have piled on--we are trying to get to the core of ourselves," Kathleen Gallagher believes.

In accompanying annual pilgrimages since 1977, Father Joseph Allen, O.P., has advised travelers to remember that a pilgrimage consists not only of prayer and penance but also play. The sick and those who come alongside them at Lourdes, Father Allen says, should find joy in the journey and the company.

That spirit of joy, Father Clinton Zadroga would agree, simply belongs to Lourdes. "Bernadette had it in the midst of trials and tribulations, trying to convince people that this was really happening," he says, "and after that with her experience of the cross in her religious life." Father Clint sees that joy among pilgrims today. "One of the most beautiful fruits of Lourdes," he says, "is joy."

chapter four

·   •   ·

SPECIAL GROUPS OF PILGRIMS, THOSE WHO SUFFER IN BODY, mind or spirit, have long made the trek to Lourdes. They arrived at first in small numbers, often in the company of family or friends. By the late nineteenth century, a contingent of the sick and dying were typically part of the large-scale national pilgrimages making their way to Lourdes. While the mode of transportation today varies, most of the large pilgrimages bring together the sick in tandem with those who offer physical, spiritual, material and moral support.

The journey to Lourdes has required sacrifice for both the sick and the volunteers. Coming by train in the early years, the sick, many of them invalids, waited on stretchers at station platforms and endured the intense summer heat of the train cars. Upon their arrival they waited once again until volunteers could carry them in their arms or by cart, chair or mattress to the grotto. At the same time the volunteers, stepping outside of their own lives and routines, took on the arduous responsibilities of nursing, feeding and transporting the sick in their charge. Even for today's pilgrims who have special needs, going on a pilgrimage to Lourdes exacts a toll.

Brother James E. O'Brien, O.F.M. CONV., wears several hats. He teaches nursing and serves as community infirmarian for the Conventual Franciscan Friars of Marytown, located north of Chicago. And each year he accompanies the U.S. National Rosary Pilgrimage to Lourdes as a staff nurse. In this latter role he sees close up the demands that international travel places on both the well and the sick.

An eight-hour transatlantic flight to Paris, followed by a connecting flight to southern France and then a bus ride to Lourdes can exhaust any traveler, Brother Jim says, but especially those with serious health problems. "We can get up, we can move around, we can use the bathroom as we need." Imagine the trip, he suggests, from the vantage point of a pilgrim who has special needs. "When someone is ill, unable to walk, in pain or having difficulty breathing, it is a grueling journey of faith."

The faith of the sick and suffering inspires not only Brother Jim but also other members of the pilgrimage. "Everybody helps each other. We don't know each other until we start on this pilgrimage," he says. "We become a family. That's the grace that God accords us."

Throughout its history Lourdes has hosted pilgrimages of individuals who share the same illness or disability and their caregivers. For example, the Crusade for the Blind Pilgrimage first came in the 1940s, and the Polio Pilgrimage arrived in the 1960s. The latter continues to this day, with its ranks filled with people who have other debilitating diseases.

Faith and Light went to Lourdes in 1971, the first of several pilgrimages the international organization would make there. Jean Vanier, the founder of L'Arche, and Marie Hélène Mathieu began Faith and Light in response to a request from two children with developmental learning disabilities and their parents. The first Faith and Light pilgrimage brought together 12,000 people from fifteen countries, including 4,000 children, teens and adults with special needs. They assembled at the grotto on Easter Sunday. Lourdes served up an opportunity for all to share friendship and encouragement and, at the same time, foster acceptance among other pilgrims, many of whom had little or no understanding of individuals with mental handicaps.

During 2001, the year of the organization's thirtieth anniversary, more than 16,000 Faith and Light pilgrims representing nearly eighty countries came to Lourdes. The movement had by this time branched out from its Catholic roots to include members of other Christian faiths. Pope John Paul II sent a letter from the Vatican, welcoming the ecumenical group gathered in Lourdes. "The presence together in Lourdes of different Christian confessions, Catholic, Orthodox, Anglican and Protestant, testifies on the basis of your common faith in the Risen Christ, that every individual is a gift from God, with inalienable dignity and rights," the pope wrote.[1]

Recognizing that each person is a gift from God--no matter what his or her faith, nationality, age, race or health condition--is the business of the Sanctuary of Our Lady of Lourdes, also called the Domain. Here people with infirmities are embraced and loved. The staff and volunteers refer to this as giving to the sick and suffering their "pride of place." This means that throughout the Domain they come first--first in line, first in procession, first in accommodations and, importantly, first in the hearts and minds of staff, volunteers and other pilgrims.

The Sanctuary of Our Lady of Lourdes invites individuals with special needs along with their caregivers to stay at the Accueil

Notre-Dame. The French word *accueil*, which means "welcome," helps to define the nature of the Accueil Notre-Dame. Neither a hotel nor a hospital, the *accueil* is home to approximately 900 pilgrims at any given time during pilgrimage season. The *accueil* serves as a residential base from which caregivers and volunteers assist the pilgrims in visiting the grotto, going into the baths and participating in the processions and sacramental celebrations.

The modern Accueil Notre-Dame stands five stories high. Situated on the right bank of the River Gave across from the Chapel of Reconciliation, the Accueil Notre-Dame is just a short distance from the grotto.

Another *accueil*, the Accueil Marie Saint Frai, operated by the Daughters of Our Lady of Sorrows, is just minutes south of the Domain, not far from the Gate of Saint Joseph. Both *accueils* provide spacious, light-filled environments. The staff and a corps of volunteers combine efforts to provide compassionate care and service throughout the pilgrims' stay. Physicians are on call; rooms are equipped with monitors and oxygen; customized meals meet the dietary needs and tastes of the international guests; and gathering areas provide places for the sick, their caregivers and others to socialize.

Chapels within the *accueils* help the sick and their companions enter more fully into the spirit of Lourdes. After a busy day, Sister Maria-Paulina Sterling appreciated going to the chapel to pray for others. "There were people I met on pilgrimage who needed spiritual help with many of the difficult things in their lives," she recalls.

Other residences designated for the sick and those with special needs are the Salus Infirmorum, located near the Gate of Saint Michael and owned by UNITALSI, the Italian pilgrimage group;

and Hosanna House, owned by British pilgrimage group HCPT and located outside of Lourdes near Bartrès. In addition, many pilgrims who have special needs stay at the hotels in town, assisted by members of their pilgrimage group. No matter where the sick reside, they are the esteemed guests of the Sanctuary of Our Lady of Lourdes. For some of these pilgrims, the shrine of Our Lady of Lourdes stands as a last hope; for many others, respite and renewal.

"Lourdes is the beacon for sickness and for illness," says Basilian Father Thomas Rosica, the chief executive officer of the Salt and Light Catholic Television Network in Canada and the past national director of World Youth Day 2002 in Toronto. "There are places that make a reality concrete," he says. "The reality that has been made concrete in Lourdes is the whole mystery of suffering."

As Father Rosica suggests, suffering is not an abstraction at Lourdes. In fact, Father Rosica's own vocation to the priesthood was influenced in part by the suffering he witnessed there. As a young university student taking classes and working in France during the summers, Father Rosica capped off his studies by volunteering at Lourdes. Each day he helped transport the sick from the *accueils* to the baths and the grotto.

"When you do that all day long for a couple of weeks," he says, "it gets to you." Seeing parents who, against all odds, tenderly brought their sick children to the grotto in hopes of a cure especially moved him. "You see the massive dose of sickness and suffering but also the healing power of Lourdes that was there—not so much through the miraculous healings as through the transformation of faith," Father Rosica recalls. It is that transformation of faith that rests in the heart of the mystery of suffering.

In the company of so many at Lourdes who are infirm in body, mind or spirit, one cannot help but wonder why. Why must this person suffer so? In his letter to the Church "On the Christian Meaning of Human Suffering" (*Salvifici Doloris*), Pope John Paul II said that God has given the answer to this question in the cross of Jesus Christ. Suffering, the pope wrote on the Feast of Our Lady of Lourdes in 1984, is above all a calling or a vocation. "Christ does not explain in the abstract the reasons for suffering, but before all else he says: 'Follow me!' Come! Take part through your suffering in this work of saving the world, a salvation achieved through my suffering! Through my Cross." When we pick up our cross and unite ourselves to the cross of Christ, the pope explained, the redemptive meaning of suffering reveals itself.[2]

Through the example of Christ, man learns "*to do good by his suffering* and *to do good to those who suffer.*"[3] It is that exchange—accomplishing good through uniting one's suffering with Christ and offering good works to those who suffer—that visitors see manifested at Lourdes.

Katie Patton, a student from Franciscan University in Steubenville, Ohio, served as a volunteer in the baths at Lourdes. She speaks passionately about the mutual love she witnessed between those who were sick and those who assisted them at the shrine. "In going to Lourdes, you really see the beauty and dignity that rightfully belongs to every single person, especially those who are suffering." This stands in contrast, she says, to the way in which our larger society all too often dismisses those who are weak or diminished. "People think if you're suffering, your life is worth nothing.

"The people who were suffering were such strong witnesses of

Christ, especially those who were suffering and did it with a smile," according to Katie. "Those are the people in whom you can see the redemptive element that belongs to suffering. Lourdes helps to cultivate that and helps you to realize that people who are suffering and dying *are* people."

Embodied in the sick and the suffering is a lesson for everyone. "Instead of running from them, you should be running to them and seeing what it is that they can teach you," Katie says. "When you learn how to deal with suffering and learn of the dignity and grace that are in death, that's when you're learning to live."

Bradley Edward Fallon taught such a lesson. When he died at thirty-six years of age, he left behind his expectant wife, Victoria, and six children, Veronica, Joseph, Louis, John, Anthony and Ignatius. The couple's youngest child—Bradley Edward Angelo Thomas Marie Fallon—entered the world just weeks after his father was buried. Victoria named him for the father he would never know (Bradley Edward), with the name Brad felt inspired to call his unborn son after leaving Mass one morning (Angelo), for the great saint on whose feast day Brad had died (Thomas Aquinas) and for the Mother of God (Marie), to whom Brad devoted himself all his life. Holding her youngest son, who is now two years old, on her lap, Victoria simply calls him Angelo. Her loss is still too recent, she says, to call him by the name he shares with her late husband.

In one of those coincidences that seem more heavenly inspired than happenstance, Victoria spoke of Lourdes seven years to the week after the couple's visit there. She marks the date on her calendar each year so that she and her family might remember.

Brad Fallon's kidneys failed not long after the couple married in 1991. A transplant in 1994 offered hope. A second transplant in

1999 renewed that hope, if only for a short time. While Brad's work at a local university was coming to an end, a new job in a different city was in the works. Then the hospital called.

The biopsy, they told Brad, revealed that the disease had returned and at an accelerated rate. Hearing the word *reoccurrence* uttered by her husband, Victoria remembers saying aloud, "Praised be Jesus Christ."

"What more was there to say?" she asks. "So much of our sufferings are our own fault because we have our sinfulness, our problems and our own baggage. Some suffering—like this suffering—just seems divine. It was as if God was calling our family to it."

By the time the dust settled, Victoria says, Brad had lost his kidney and was receiving dialysis. The job under discussion had vanished. "They didn't want him. His health was not predictable at that point," she says.

A religious order offered to send Brad and Victoria along with their newest baby, Anthony, to Lourdes during 2000, the year of the Great Jubilee of the Church. Victoria remembers wondering what her husband would say in response to this offer. While his health was rapidly deteriorating, "he never chased doctors or apparitions." He knew God could heal him from anywhere if it were his will. Brad surprised her when he said he wanted to go. "Our Lady is calling me to Lourdes," he said.

Victoria remembers looking out the window of their room at the Accueil Notre-Dame, shortly after checking in, and seeing a steady stream of the sick and volunteers making their way from the *accueils* to the grotto. "It was like the candlelight procession, but more beautiful because it was all the sick people," Victoria remembers. "And here we were; *we* were these sick people."

Embracing that realization amounted to a sea change for Victoria, who before her husband's health began its steep decline never felt quite at home in the company of people who were ill. "There was love in this procession of people, in the people lining them up, in the people pushing them on their carts and wheelchairs. Being in a place where the sick are honored like that helped me see what an honor it was for me to be with my husband." Calling her husband to the window, she said to him, "Brad, come and look at all these people out here. Look how much our Lord loves the sick."

Later Victoria toured the town, while Brad went to the St. John the Baptist Dialysis Centre nearby. Instead of complaining about the time it took away from his pilgrimage, Brad expressed thanks for the outstanding view of the Pyrénées its wall of windows afforded him.

Victoria was at the same time contemplating a different view—that of the *cachot*, the old jail in which Bernadette's family had lived. Standing in the single room that had housed all six Soubirous family members, Victoria felt a great weight fall from her shoulders. She thought of Brad's health, the family's loss of their sole provider, the uncertainty of their finances and the sacrifices that she, her husband and children would have to make. She felt for the first time not overwhelmed but comforted.

"Not only is the *cachot* small, poor and humble, but they say a dung hill was right outside their window," Victoria explains. "These people—the Soubirous family—they didn't have a lot going for them. And that's how I felt about us."

As she further surveyed the living accommodations, Victoria realized that in spite of the Soubirous family's poverty, God had blessed them beyond measure in the Blessed Virgin's appearing to Bernadette. "I had to trust. I just felt at peace in that *cachot* that God would take care of us too," she remembers. "God had this in his hands. God knew from the beginning that all these things would happen, and of course, he would take care of us."

All three of the Fallons went to the baths. "The men's line is always shorter. With the women's line, you're back six decades of the rosary," recalls Victoria. Calling "the lady with the baby," the volunteers moved her and four-month-old Anthony to the head of the line.

Brad bathed on the other side. "Certainly he could have stepped out of that water and been totally healed. That would have been beautiful," his widow says softly. "Sometimes—not sometimes, but often—the better healing is a deeper, more personal healing. It's an acceptance." Bradley Fallon, his wife believes, discovered in Lourdes the reason Mary had invited him there.

Beneath the photo of her husband that hangs in the family's living room is a small shelf. A wrist chain rests on it. Holding it in her hand, Victoria says, "Saint Louis de Montfort talks about wearing outward signs for your consecration to Jesus through Mary. Brad wore this chain for almost our whole marriage. At the end he had to take it off because it was ruining one of his veins that he needed for dialysis."

The chain symbolizes for Victoria the deep devotion her husband had to Mary, a devotion that began as a child when he regularly prayed the rosary, a devotion that opened his heart to the message he received at Lourdes. "Mary was calling him to be stronger, to be better and to carry his burdens," Victoria says of his experience there. Mary was inviting the young husband and father to shoulder the cross for her Son.

In the next few years, God blessed the Fallons with another son,

Ignatius, who has Down Syndrome. They continued to home school their children and delighted in learning side by side with them. Brad now suffered from both advanced kidney disease and congestive heart failure and was unable to work. In the midst of this, a religious sister, a friend, bathed in the waters of Lourdes on his behalf. That very day, he told his wife, he experienced a joy he had never known—a joy that went far beyond the happiness that his family and life had always brought him.

Not long after—on Christmas Day 2004—Brad received a special and unexpected gift, a new kidney. The family breathed a sigh of relief when he returned home to recover, but his stay was only temporary. On January 28, 2005, Brad Fallon died of septic shock, an outcome of the failed kidney transplant.

"Brad had suffering. He took it. He embraced it. He took more. He loved more through it. And he learned more by it," Victoria Fallon says in recalling her husband's last years. "I was very proud of my husband."

One day Victoria hopes that she and her seven children might travel to Lourdes. There they can experience together the place that, according to Victoria, so beautifully strengthened her beloved husband for his final healing, his death.

Long before John Paul II wrote his letter on human suffering, he was a man well acquainted with pain. His words, works and very presence testified clearly to this mystery of suffering, as much an integral part of his life as it is the landscape of Lourdes. Karol Wojtyla lost his mother, brother and father before he turned twenty-one. After the Nazis occupied Poland and closed the universities, he worked as a laborer and attended a clandestine seminary to prepare for the priesthood.

In 1981, the third year of his reign as pope, he was severely wounded in an assassination attempt in St. Peter's Square. Mehmet Ali Aga, a twenty-three-year-old Turk, fired three shots at close range into the pontiff's abdomen, left hand and right arm. The pope had to cancel his plan to attend the International Eucharistic Congress in Lourdes later that summer.

For the Feast of the Assumption in 1983, John Paul II, appearing recovered and robust, arrived in Lourdes. During the procession of the Blessed Sacrament, he addressed the many sick and suffering present. "You who are ill, I would like you to keep in your hearts and minds three small lights that seem to me very precious," he told the assembled crowd.[4]

These "lights" that the pope offered in guiding the sick on their pathway of suffering were awareness, acceptance and oblation. The first consists of being fully aware of one's suffering—physical, moral, personal or familial—without minimizing it or exaggerating it and the effects it has. The next, he explained, is accepting the fact that things are what they are and believing that the Lord can draw good from evil. Then comes, the pope said, "the finest gesture...yet to be made: that of oblation"—offering one's suffering in union with Christ's suffering.

"These three stages, lived by each suffering person according to his or her rhythm or grace, give rise to an astonishing interior liberation," John Paul II said.[5] In losing one's life for Christ's sake, the pope reminded the sick, they will find it (see Matthew 16:25). He told the sick and suffering that to understand this they need look no further than to the daughters of nineteenth-century France— Bernadette of Lourdes and Thérèse of Lisieux, who were both sick most of their lives.

When John Paul II returned to Lourdes as pontiff and pilgrim in 2004, his final foreign apostolic trip, the world could see that these "three precious lights" that he had once recommended to the sick now guided his unsteady walk. Father Thomas Rosica remembers vividly the moment in the grotto when John Paul II gave one of his finest lessons on the meaning of suffering. "What John Paul did there in August 2004 was remarkable," he says. He explains that the pope allowed himself to be a spectacle to the world.

Father Rosica recalls working that weekend in the master control room of the new studios of the Salt and Light Catholic Television Network in Toronto. Glancing at two monitors, he noticed that two very different dramas were unfolding.

"One television network was airing scenes of the Olympic Games from Athens—featuring and exalting the human body in its youthfulness, agility, and beauty," Father Rosica would later tell a group of students and members of the University of Toronto Catholic community. "Another monitor carried scenes of quite a different theater unfolding at a famous Catholic shrine tucked away in the Pyrénées in southern France—featuring not sportsmanship and physique as in Athens, but diminishment, suffering, disfigurement and pain that are so much a part of the pilgrimage center at Lourdes." At the center of these latter scenes, Father Rosica continued, was "an 84-year-old pontiff, slumped over on his kneeler as he prayed before the image of the Blessed Mother."[6]

After first greeting the sick, the Holy Father was too spent to continue speaking. Cardinal Roger Etchegaray read on his behalf: "Dear brothers and sisters who are sick, how I would like to embrace each and every one of you with affection, to tell you how close I am to you and how much I support you."[7] Both suffering servant and Good Samaritan, the pope was very much at home in the Grotto of Massabielle.

Brad Fallon, former theology instructor and father of seven, and Pope John Paul II, chief theologian and spiritual father to more than one billion sons and daughters throughout the world, both died of septic shock in the same year. They are but two of the countless pilgrims who are numbered among the past, present and future communities of the sick and the suffering at Lourdes.

Each day many of these pilgrims join in the Blessed Sacrament procession at Lourdes. Introduced by Assumptionist Father François Picard, the first procession occurred on August 22, 1888. For more than 100 years, it has been part of the daily life of Lourdes. From April to mid-October, pilgrims gather at 5:00 PM every day, either in front of the open-air altar on the prairie across from the grotto or in the underground Basilica of St. Pius X. Many of the sick elect to wait in the basilica because of their infirmities or to avoid the summer heat.

Just before the procession begins, a deacon brings the large monstrance from the Tent of Adoration to the altar in the field. The monstrance, from the Latin word *monstrare*, meaning "to show," is a sacred vessel that displays the consecrated host, the Body and Blood, soul and divinity of Jesus Christ. The Lourdes monstrance has a huge circular window covering the equally large sacred host.

The procession begins from the outdoor altar. At the head of the procession is a pilgrim—often in a wheelchair—carrying the banner of the Sanctuary of Our Lady of Lourdes. Other banner and flag carriers representing the different pilgrimage groups follow. The sick once again enjoy pride of place, taking the front positions. Priests from all over the world, dressed in their white albs and stoles, march together. Pilgrims carrying incense signal that Christ is near.

Under a canopy the bishop or priest carries the Blessed Sacrament in the monstrance, surrounded by pilgrims carrying banners of angels. Visiting physicians and nurses who have accompanied the pilgrimage groups bring up the rear of this procession; the medical director of Lourdes processes with them. Dominican Father Joseph Allen says the procession comforts the sick and the well. "Christ walks among his people," he says.

The people of God make their way to the Basilica of St. Pius X. The pilgrims who have opted to wait in the underground basilica witness the procession on the large screens there. The blessing of the sick now takes place. "One lead *brancardier*—the old term for what we now call a 'stretcher-bearer'—accompanies the priest carrying the monstrance and 'introduces' him to the group to be blessed by a wave of his hand in a sweeping motion," Brother Jim O'Brien, O.F.M. CONV., explains. Several volunteer stretcher-bearers and physicians follow the priest, who blesses the sick with the monstrance. For Brother Jim this is a moving moment of the service.

"Christ leads the way," he says. "Having the doctors trailing behind makes us aware that God is the Divine Physician, but he watches over our doctors here on Earth who are entrusted with the care of his sick!"

Dr. Michael Martinelli remembers the time he was chosen randomly by the chief physician of the shrine to be a part of the blessing of the sick. While acknowledging that physicians are instruments of God in improving the lives of the sick and making them more comfortable in their illnesses, Dr. Martinelli says the experience reinforced for him the fact that the spiritual transformations of Lourdes are much more profound than the physical cures. Here where pilgrims say yes to Mary's invitation to come in procession, they draw closer to her Son.

Many people who suffer physically, mentally or spiritually may never have the opportunity to visit Lourdes. A bridge of faith, however, unites them to this shrine of healing. John Paul II laid the foundations of this bridge when he established in 1992 the World Day of the Sick. It is to be commemorated each year on February 11, the Feast of Our Lady of Lourdes, "whose shrine at the foot of the Pyrénées has become a temple of suffering."[8]

The pope urged that the day be a time of praying and sharing, offering one's suffering for the good of the Church and recognizing Christ in the face of the sick. The pope hoped that the World Day of the Sick might energize governments, scientists and health care providers to make health care more widely available and more compassionate. While commemorated worldwide, its centralized site of celebration moves each year from one continent to another. Lourdes hosted the Twelfth World Day of the Sick in 2004, which coincided with the 150th anniversary of the declaration of the dogma of the Immaculate Conception.

"If Jesus is the source of life that conquers death, Mary is the attentive mother who comes to meet the needs of her children, obtaining for them the health of soul and body," John Paul II wrote for that occasion. While many sick and suffering have been restored to physical health through the intercession of Our Lady of Lourdes, even more surprising miracles occur. "The Holy Spirit, who covered her with his shadow at the moment of the Incarnation of the Word, transforms the souls of countless sick people who turn to her," the pope wrote. "Even when they do not obtain the gift of bodily health, they are able to receive another that is much more important: the conversion of heart, source of peace and interior joy."[9]

chapter five

. . • . .

HOSPITALITY

AN INTERNATIONAL HOTEL CHAIN ADVERTISES, "HOSPITALITY is spoken here."[1] Lourdes matches and betters that claim. Hospitality is lived out each and every day.

The Hospitality Association of Our Lady of Lourdes, an arch-confraternity of the Catholic Church, was formed in 1885 to receive and assist an increasing number of pilgrims journeying to Lourdes. The association comes under the authority of the bishop of Tarbes and Lourdes. It is, in a sense, an international family with more than 200 "daughter" hospitalities around the globe. Each was founded by and serves at the pleasure of the local ordinary or the superior of a religious order. All are affiliated with the "mother" archconfraternity in Lourdes and its bishop.

Today more than eight thousand Hospitality volunteers come annually to serve at Lourdes. They pay for their own transportation, accommodations and meals in exchange for the privilege of helping pilgrims they do not know. These volunteers, *les hospitaliers* and *les hospitalières*, complete a five-year formal program consisting of a week of annual service, training and spiritual formation at Lourdes. While in training the Hospitality volunteers are known as *stagiares:* They are at various "stages" of apprenticing or interning. During their fifth year of service, they pledge to welcome pilgrims to the Sanctuary, especially those who are sick or have special needs, and to pass on to them the message of Lourdes.

Father Régis-Marie de La Teyssonnière knows intimately the hearts of those who volunteer at Lourdes. Before his international assignment as roving ambassador coupled with his appointment as a spiritual director and liaison for North American Lourdes Volunteers, he served for nine years as chaplain general of the Hospitality of Our Lady of Lourdes. In that role Father de La Teyssonnière offered spiritual guidance to the thousands of volunteers and the hundreds of seminarians who come annually to assist in welcoming and serving pilgrims at Lourdes.

Father de La Teyssonnière believes that many who volunteer at Lourdes do so in response to the same mysterious invitation that Bernadette received. Our Lady asked Bernadette, "Would you be so kind as to come here for fifteen days?" "With this invitation to come," Father de La Teyssonnière suggests, "the grace—that is to say, the capacity—is given."

The volunteers see firsthand the results of their service. "The fruits are the fruits of the holy cross, the fruits given as signs of the kingdom of heaven: love, peace and joy," Father de La Teyssonnière says. While Lourdes needs both general volunteers and volunteers with particular sets of skills, the most important qualification, he says, is to be a "specialist of humanity" in all aspects: body, heart, spirit and soul.

The first Hospitality in the Americas was born in the third millennium.

For four days in 2001, Marlene Watkins, a homemaker from Syracuse, New York, waited with two sick women in a lengthy line at the famous baths. On the fourth day, which was Ascension Thursday, she grew concerned that her two companions might once again be turned away because of the crowd. She approached the entry and explained the situation to the attendant. There followed an exchange in which the attendant noted Marlene's capability. Marlene was ushered inside the baths and asked to help. She was surprised to learn that few of the women assisting spoke English.

At the end of the day, humbled by the profound experience of service, Marlene knelt, kissed the floor and promised Our Lady that she would return to Lourdes with ten American women volunteers. A year later she came back with nine other laywomen, a layman and a priest from Canada. These "North American Lourdes Volunteers" gave a week of service to the sick and suffering. Marlene was invited to form the first American Hospitality as a private association.

In 2003 the Hospitality of Our Lady of Lourdes urged the North American Lourdes Volunteers to place their apostolate under the authority of the bishop of Syracuse, the Most Reverend James Moynihan. After the formal period of observation, on June 10, 2005, Bishop Moynihan raised Our Lady of Lourdes Hospitality North American Lourdes Volunteers to a public association of the Christian faithful under canon law. He praised the group for evangelizing through a mission of charity and love.

In its short lifespan, North American Lourdes Volunteers has inspired more than a thousand volunteers throughout the United States, Canada, Mexico and the Caribbean Islands to become Hospitality *stagiaires* at Lourdes or to accompany those with special needs on their pilgrimages to the grotto. In addition to its general appeal for volunteers, the association has successfully reached out to members of the military and college students. North American Lourdes Volunteers believe it's critical to include the young. Recognizing that Bernadette was only fourteen when Our Lady revealed herself at the Grotto of Massabielle, the North American Lourdes Volunteers also sponsor catechesis pilgrimages for students between the ages of fourteen and seventeen. These students live and learn their faith by assisting where needed at Lourdes.

The mission of the North American Lourdes Volunteers is "to extend the invitation of the Immaculate Conception as given to Bernadette in the grotto at Lourdes, to serve the sick and suffering at Lourdes and at home following the loving example of Saint Bernadette in simplicity, humility and obedience." Service at home includes conducting talks and retreats on Lourdes and the spirituality of Saint Bernadette. The association sponsors a "virtual pilgrimage," a ninety-minute presentation for parishes, schools, nursing homes, monasteries and prisons. The "pilgrims in spirit" hear the message of Lourdes, participate in a Eucharistic procession, wash in water from the spring, touch a piece of rock taken from the grotto and experience an abbreviated torchlight procession while reciting a decade of the rosary.

Marlene Watkins believes strongly that Mary places the desire to serve in the hearts of volunteers. "Our Lady has the passenger manifest," Marlene says, "She knows whom she is calling. Our Lady calls us to serve her and her pilgrims at Lourdes as a blessing to us and not just a blessing to those we serve."

Sometimes recognizing the inner desire to volunteer takes a little work. A group of students from Franciscan University of Steubenville laugh when they recall passing by a North American

Lourdes Volunteers sign posted at their satellite campus in Austria. "Is Mary Calling You?" the sign asked. Steve Mierendorf, a theology major from Michigan, says, "I remember very specifically saying, 'No!'" It was just a matter of time, according to Steve, before he felt a tugging at his heart and signed up to volunteer over spring break.

Nate Lauer's initial response to the call to service was also a no. Nate, who hails from Colorado and majors in theology and German, had no desire to give up his vacation plans. He attributes his turnaround to the graces of a Marian consecration he had recently made.

Katie Patton of Pennsylvania turned to prayer before the Blessed Sacrament in making her decision. "I sometimes have a hard time hearing what God calls me to do," the catechetics and theology major says. When Katie learned at the informational meeting that the "sick and the pilgrims are treated like royalty" at Lourdes, she knew she was called to serve.

The North American Lourdes Volunteers typically serve in the baths; in the special residential places of welcome for the sick—the Accueil Marie Saint-Frai and the Accueil Notre-Dame—where they help with housekeeping chores and meals; and in the Service of St. Joseph. The latter service engages men in managing the arrival and departure of the sick and those with special needs at the Lourdes train station and airports, lifting them out of the trains or transit. They also organize processions and welcome pilgrims at the baths.

The volunteer or *stagiare* experience at Lourdes can be physically demanding, humbling and even socially isolating, since English-speaking volunteers are in the minority. But few would exchange it for anything in the world.

Nate Lauer says that serving at Lourdes during Holy Week heightened his understanding of the relationship of Christ's suffering to the suffering of the world. Having witnessed so many people struggling in the baths and at the station, where he helped the sick board trains, Nate realized that the world often asks how a loving God can allow so much pain. The experience at Lourdes made him realize that at some point each of us will suffer mentally or physically, and we must call on the Lord.

"I never appreciated the face of suffering," he says. "If I have taken anything away, I feel there's a little part of my heart always reserved for lenten repentance because of Lourdes." In being present to those with special needs and sorrows, Nate says, he realized that the world is not picture perfect and is still "in need of the Savior who came already."

In serving in the baths during Holy Week, Steve Mierendorf discovered that he actually had the privilege of doing what Christ commanded when he said at the Last Supper, "If I then, your Lord and Teacher, have washed your feet, you also ought to wash one another's" (John 13:14). Steve and the other volunteers used the long aprons they wore to dry the feet of older men after they had bathed. He expresses gratitude in being able to humbly give that gift, as well as appreciation of the men's humility in receiving it. According to Steve, "It was an amazing experience to do that service, especially for a brother of mine whom I didn't know and couldn't communicate with but could still love."

A similar experience happened in the women's baths. Katie Patton describes how the volunteers "would drop to their knees" to help elderly women put their socks or stockings on. "Being able to be there, to hold someone's hand or just be present to them and let them know you are there to love and serve them," Katie says, "was an honor." Step by step, Katie believes, serving at Lourdes led her to a deeper love of God and others over self.

Finding Christ in the "other" was also a grace that Danielle Castellucci from Ohio received. A senior majoring in mental health and human services, Danielle recalls the first time a pilgrim on a stretcher came into the baths while she was there.

"I was asked to hold the woman as they were undressing her," Danielle says. "I was holding this woman in my arms and was overwhelmed with her beauty." The face she gazed at, Danielle found, was "the face of Christ." The experience of serving changed her. "Lourdes is and always will be," according to Danielle, "the home of my heart." It was there, she says, that she discovered her "vocation to love."

Ellen McMahon, a senior education major from New York, went to Lourdes during her sophomore year at Franciscan University. In looking back on that experience, she recalls how difficult the work could be in the baths. "That was more grueling than anything I had ever done in my life. I was wet. My hands were chapped and raw because of the cold water." Being around very sick people was also a new experience for her.

Ellen admits that when she went to Lourdes, her devotion to Mary was in its budding stage, and she had been nourishing it only halfheartedly. "Volunteering at Lourdes was the turning point in my adulthood," she notes. "After Lourdes Our Lady was an absolute, a real presence in my life, and her Son was the lover of my soul."

Ellen also was awed by working near the grotto. Where else on your way to work, she wonders, can you pass by the very spot where Mary appeared? It was there that Ellen comforted a sobbing elderly Italian woman. The barriers of language, age and culture melted away as each reached out to the other. Opening her Bible randomly after her new friend left, Ellen was blessed to read, "How beautiful you are, how pleasing,/my love, my delight" (Song of Songs 7:7, NAB). There could be no better thank you for volunteering than that.

Deacon Tom Kinnick of the diocese of La Crosse, Wisconsin, places service at Lourdes in the context of the cross. "We are looking for a way for the cross to make sense in our lives," the recently ordained permanent deacon says. It only makes sense, he says, when we recognize the intersection of its two dimensions. The vertical beam symbolizes the praise, honor and glory due to God. The horizontal beam represents how we live out our daily lives as Christians.

"In Lourdes we give that perfect praise, honor and glory to God the Father through serving the poor, the sick, the marginalized, the ill and the handicapped." For Deacon Kinnick, who serves as youth ministry director for the deanery of Chippewa Falls, Lourdes gives teens and young adults from his diocese the opportunity to step up and "be what they are called to be"—that is, sharers in the mission of Jesus Christ, the salvation of the world. "This is accomplished by loving as Christ loved—the fruit of which is the service of our brothers and sisters," says Deacon Kinnick.

The privilege of service encourages Theresa Stiner, a mother, grandmother and computer troubleshooter, to return with the North American Lourdes Volunteers each year. She recognizes that she assists not only in a practical way but also spiritually. "You're helping pilgrims participate in a once-in-a-lifetime experience, which brings them closer to God and Mary," she says. Service, for Theresa, is prayer in action. "When we are attending the pilgrims, that is our prayer."

People not affiliated with any particular organization or group sometimes apply directly to the Hospitality Association of Our Lady of Lourdes to volunteer. Manuel and Melinda Henson of Chicago did just that. Melinda says that neither she nor her husband had ever given much thought to visiting a shrine, let alone offering their services at one. When a dear friend, a physician, was diagnosed with cancer, she asked Melinda if she would accompany her to Lourdes. Before they were able to make the journey, the woman died. "My husband and I decided to go in her honor," Melinda recalls.

This year, their fifth year of volunteering, they will make their commitment to the Hospitality and confirm this service as a commitment to the Church during a Mass in the Sanctuary of Our Lady of Lourdes. At that time they will receive a silver medal with the image of the Blessed Virgin attached to a blue and white ribbon featuring the cross of Saint Peter. This cross is upside down, representing the way in which Saint Peter was crucified and symbolizing the humility required of *hospitaliers*.

The Our Lady of Lourdes insignia is a sign of dedication, the Hospitality is quick to point out, not a decoration. It telegraphs that the wearer, a member of the Hospitality of Our Lady of Lourdes, has pledged to serve the sick and, in a special way, all those who come to Lourdes.

Over the five years that Melinda has volunteered, she has arranged flowers for the chapels, washed dishes, swept floors, polished elevator doors in the centers for the sick and, most recently, worked as a French translator for English-speaking pilgrims. Melinda says that no matter what she's asked to do, it doesn't seem like work but a service of love. "You're so privileged to be able to help in any way at all," she says.

Melinda and Manuel Henson's love for Our Lady and Lourdes extends beyond the time they volunteer there. Along with several friends, they launched a Web site (www.friendsoflourdesusa.com) dedicated to promoting the 150th anniversary of the apparitions of Lourdes; encouraging the more than two thousand parishes and other Catholic institutions in the United States having a name of Our Lady, Saint Bernadette or Lourdes to celebrate the jubilee; and providing tips on how to make known the message of Lourdes to friends, family and coworkers.

Many of today's members of the Hospitality Association of Our Lady of Lourdes, and in particular those from Europe, stand on the shoulders of their parents, aunts and uncles, grandparents and great grandparents who journeyed before them to Lourdes. While the French quite naturally were the first to respond in the late nineteenth century, hospitalities were formed in Great Britain, Ireland, Spain, Switzerland, Italy and Belgium as early as the 1920s and 1930s. More hospitalities would follow. One generation passed on its pilgrimage stories of faith, adventure and service to the next, which in turn was excited and humbled to carry on the tradition.

In addition to those who provide service on site at Lourdes, more than 100,000 people from throughout the world assist Lourdes and its pilgrims in another vital way. These volunteers make up what is known as the Hospitality of Accompaniment. They travel with pilgrims having special physical, psychological or emotional needs. These volunteers come from many different walks of life. Common to all is a desire to make possible for those with special needs what might, at first, seem to be the impossible.

The Sovereign Order of Saint John of Jerusalem of Rhodes and of Malta is one such organization. The Order of Malta, as it is better known, traces its founding to the eleventh century. It is the fourth oldest religious order of the Roman Catholic Church. While most of its members were vowed religious through 1800, the majority of today's 12,000 Knights and Dames of Malta are laypersons.

Present in fifty-four countries, there are three associations of the Order of Malta in the United States, including the American Association (installed 1927, with headquarters in New York City), the Western Association (1953, San Francisco) and the Federal Association (1974, Washington, D.C.). Each May thousands of members from throughout the world accompany the sick, whom they affectionately refer to by the French word *malades,* and their companions to Lourdes to participate in the International Order of Malta Lourdes Pilgrimage. Nearly a thousand Knights, Dames, volunteers, *malades* and their companions made up the total United States contingent in 2007.

Kevin White, K.M., serves currently as the Western Association Lourdes pilgrimage director. The Western Association has made the pilgrimage to Lourdes each year since 1976. "From the moment the *malades* arrive at the airport and until they return to the United States," he says, "they are cared for by the Knights and Dames of Malta."

While many of the Knights and Dames are doctors and nurses who provide medical care, all members of the order help to serve the *malades.* "The Knights and Dames push and pull the *voitures,* offer ongoing care and personal assistance whenever necessary, but most significantly they are sources of continuous love and emotional support to the *malades,*" according to Kevin. This love and support is made visible throughout the pilgrimage stay and in a particular way during the special ceremony in which the clergy, Knights and Dames wash the feet of the sick.

Dr. Paul Fallon, K.M., an oral surgeon from Syracuse, New York, is affiliated with the Federal Association. He says the commitment to service shapes the entire pilgrimage week. "We do everything not for ourselves but to serve the sick."

The daily prayer of the order, Kevin White says, inspires this compassion. It reads in part: "Be it mine to practice charity toward my neighbors, especially the poor and the sick.... Give me the strength I need to carry out this my resolve, forgetful of myself."

Jenny Schweizer, a Franciscan University student from Wisconsin, felt blessed that she could provide companionship to a woman who was blind and required a wheelchair. Each day Jenny met her assigned partner at 7:30 AM. She would push her from the Accueil Notre-Dame uphill to join the other pilgrims of the group for breakfast, then escort her back to the Domain, where together they might visit the grotto, go to the baths or participate in the planned pilgrimage events of the day.

Because the woman could not see, Jenny became her eyes. She grew to be expert in describing the churches, the crowds and the statues of Lourdes. "It was not easy at all," she says of her service. "It was physically and emotionally draining. I remember being exhausted." In the process, though, she and her pilgrimage partner formed a friendship.

Jenny has a younger sister, Nicole, who has special needs. Jenny reflects on the grace of her assignment, which allowed her not only to come alongside a pilgrim at Lourdes but also to "step into the shoes" of her mother and "see what she goes through every single day" on behalf of her sister. Lourdes confirmed for Jenny that serving is her "language of love." According to the education major, "Having that mindset helped me at Lourdes. How I show my love to God is through loving others and serving them."

Mary Dooley, a hospice nurse in upstate New York, never intended to take a busman's holiday. She first went to Lourdes not long after the death of her oldest daughter, who was in her early thirties. "I experienced a lot of healing and acceptance there after my loss," she recalls, "but that one pilgrimage to the grotto was all I ever intended."

The next year, surprising even herself, Mary returned to Lourdes, worked in the baths along with other North American Lourdes Volunteers and pledged to return. Now she goes to Lourdes for two weeks each year. She serves both in the baths as a volunteer for the Hospitality of Our Lady of Lourdes and also as head nurse for the North American Lourdes Volunteers' annual accompaniment pilgrimage for individuals with special needs.

Before the plane lifts off the ground, Mary has already invested countless hours in preparation. She interviews the pilgrims and their caregivers to determine medical needs such as oxygen, motorized wheelchair transfers and Hoyer lifts. She assesses the number of volunteers needed, plans suitable transportation and matches the unique needs of each pilgrim with the ideal accommodations and care providers. Along with the other care team members, Mary then helps support the specific needs of the pilgrims throughout their journey.

"I do similar work here," she explains, "but there is something so amazing about being in Lourdes with the sick and handicapped pilgrims, where they are given pride of place." No matter how challenging it might be to bring those with special needs to Lourdes, Mary says, it is "a rewarding privilege and joy."

Brother Jim O'Brien, O.F.M. CONV., R.N., serves as a member of the medical team for the U.S. National Rosary Pilgrimage. "As a nurse, I am so privileged, so thankful, so grateful, to have the ability to work with all these people who are sick. Some are even close to death." It is a grace, he believes, to share in their experience.

For thirty years Father Joseph Allen, O.P., has accompanied as chaplain the same U.S. National Rosary Pilgrimage. "I see my own apostolate there as sharing my charism of preaching and ministering," Father Allen says. That charism, he explains, is rooted in his own Dominican tradition and spirituality, in which members ponder, pray over and share the Word of God.

What compels these volunteers to bypass the beach or the mountains to serve Lourdes pilgrims? Pope John Paul II, in his apostolic letter "On the Christian Meaning of Human Suffering" (Salvifici Doloris), gave us a glimpse of why so many volunteers might answer Mary's call to come to Lourdes. The late pope reminded us that the gospel of suffering is not only about our suffering neighbor; it is about us. It is about our response to our brothers and our sisters who are afflicted, whether in body or soul. Our supreme model for service, the pontiff wrote, is Jesus Christ, who *drew increasingly closer to the world of human suffering.* He healed the sick, restored sight and hearing and freed those in bondage to sin. He raised the dead to life. He took *this suffering upon his very self.* And by means of his ultimate suffering on the cross, he accomplished the work of salvation.[2]

The parable of the Good Samaritan, John Paul II further taught, belongs to this same gospel of suffering. Christ used this parable to answer the question "Who is my neighbor?" Three men—a priest, a Levite and a Samaritan—spy a man who lies beaten by robbers and left for dead on the road to Jericho. The priest and Levite pass by on the other side; it is only the Samaritan who stops and takes pity. He bandages the man's wounds and takes him to an inn. The Samaritan entrusts him to the care of the innkeeper. He promises to return and pay any expenses spent on the injured man's recovery.

The story, according to John Paul II, epitomizes what Christ intends our relationship to be toward our suffering neighbor. *"Everyone who stops beside the suffering of another person,* whatever form it may take," John Paul II wrote, "is a Good Samaritan. This stopping does not mean curiosity but availability."[3] It is availability that presses beyond compassion that one sees at work at Lourdes.

Wringing out a sheet in the baths, wiping a floor in the places for the sick or sharing a laugh with a fellow pilgrim who might need some extra help are only a few of the ways in which volunteers make themselves available. This self-donation comes with the recognition that the roles could be reversed at a later time. But for now, like the Good Samaritan, the men, women and teens that serve at Lourdes move beyond compassion to action.

When asked in what ways volunteering changes lives, Father de La Teyssonnière, a Chaplain of Honor at Lourdes, first likes to set the stage. "Sometimes people say that because you are a saint, you go often to Lourdes," he suggests. "It is exactly the contrary. It is because you go to Lourdes that you will be on your way to holiness, which is the common vocation of all Christians."

In short, volunteering does not make Christians exceptional but makes them "normal" in the purest sense of conforming to what God calls them to be. "We are all created by God to give our life to him in serving others. Entering that kind of experience touches something very deep in each of us," according to Father de La Teyssonnière. "We really are created to love, that is, to prefer others to ourselves and to demonstrate it through serving others."

Father de La Teyssonnière readily offers to volunteers and pilgrims three role models who emptied themselves for others: Jesus Christ, the servant of God, who "came not to be served but to serve" (Matthew 20:28); the Blessed Virgin, who identified herself as "the servant of the Lord" (Luke 1:38, NRSV); and Bernadette. In loving concretely through action, Father de La Teyssonnière believes, volunteers live more intensely their call to holiness, and as a result their relationships with God and with others change for the better.

Many voices in today's competitive society attempt to counter or silence Christ's call to give without counting the cost, both at Lourdes and at home. "The world teaches us to be selfish, to be successful more than to take care of others, to be better than others," Father de La Teyssonnière says. "It is not the gospel! It is not the way of life in the kingdom of heaven."

Nor is this self-absorption the way of Lourdes. "Lourdes teaches us how to love God with all our heart and to love our neighbor as ourselves. The teaching we receive at Lourdes is not only a teaching; it is at the same time a grace that makes everyone able to be successful in experiencing what is asked. That is the Good News!"

At the core of the experience is the relationship between the volunteer and the pilgrim with special needs. This relationship can be difficult from both perspectives. It needs to be nurtured with care, kindness and attention. And hidden within the center of that relationship is the paschal mystery. "Each one of us has to give his own life for the other—the volunteers for the sick and the sick for the volunteers," Father de La Teyssonnière advises.

Jenny Schweizer, the student companion to the woman who was blind, can attest to that. While acknowledging that the service she gave exhausted her. Jenny strongly believes that those requiring help sacrifice much more, for they must rely on others. "They had to ask us or tell us where they wanted to go. They had to be dependent on us," Jenny reflects. "What we did was hard, but it didn't compare to what the women we were serving were going through."

According to Father de La Teyssonnière, "The gift of oneself makes a space for Jesus in this relationship. Because of Jesus, the sick and the volunteers enter the paschal mystery, going from their own reality to the kingdom of heaven."

While this happens whenever someone gives his life for another, Father de La Teyssonnière believes that a special grace at Lourdes makes that gift evident. "At Lourdes, looking at the volunteers and the sick, millions of people are able to see the love of God manifested in the cross of Jesus Christ," he says. "In that way volunteering at Lourdes doesn't change only the life of the volunteers or the sick but also the lives of millions, making them see eternal life."

chapter six

R O C K

LOURDES TODAY WELCOMES MORE THAN 6,000,000 VISITORS A year from all over the world. In all of France, only Paris has more hotel beds than this small town tucked in the foothills of the Pyrénées.

Most visitors arrive during the main pilgrimage season, which starts in early April and extends through mid-October. Others make their way to the town of more than 17,000 during what is known as the "winter sleep," a quieter time in which visitors avoid the crowds but miss the experience of the Eucharistic and candle-light Marian processions held daily during the pilgrimage season.

Some visitors arrive at Tarbes-Lourdes-Pyrénées Airport, which is about six miles from the town, or at the slightly more distant Pau-Pyrénées Airport. Others arrive by train, charter coach, bike or car.

Many travelers who might have just glimpsed snow on the peaks of the Pyrénées on their way from the airport are surprised to find palm trees growing along the River Gave de Pau in Lourdes. This is just one of many contrasts to be found in this southwestern town, which was held at different times in its history by the French, the Moors and the English.

Sprinkled throughout the old town of Lourdes are places to be reserved for a later visit. Pilgrims are invited to "walk in the footsteps of Bernadette Soubirous to discover her message of faith."[1] A sign points to *Maison Natale de Sainte-Bernadette*, the Boly Mill that was the birthplace and childhood home of Bernadette. Pilgrims see firsthand there the simple but comfortable living quarters the family enjoyed before François Soubirous's fortunes spiraled downward in 1854.

Following the "footsteps of Bernadette" leads pilgrims to the *cachot*, the former jail cell that became the refuge for the Soubirous family in 1857. The single room of the *cachot* served as kitchen, dining room, living room and bedroom for the family of six.

Along the way pilgrims can stop at the site of the old presbytery where Bernadette confided the messages and identity of the "beautiful girl" to Father Peyramale. Other landmarks include the hospice, where the saint attended the free school, made her First Communion, lodged with the sisters and recognized her calling to be a Sister of Charity of Nevers. The town's Church of the Sacred Heart, built between 1875 and 1903, contains the font where Bernadette was baptized in the old parish church of St. Peter, which preceded it. Sun streams through the church's stained glass windows, which depict both Father Peyremale and Bernadette.

Ambitious pilgrims may hike along the pedestrian path from the town of Lourdes to the village of Bartrès. Bernadette was sent to Bartrès in November 1844 to be wet-nursed by Marie Lagües. She returned there in 1857 to work as a farm hand, babysitter and shepherdess. The sheep gate where Bernadette tended her flock, the local parish church and the home of her foster mother turned employer still exist.

While all of these landmarks help pilgrims situate Bernadette in and around Lourdes, they must wait to be visited. Those who come to Lourdes seek first, above any other site, the Grotto of Massabielle, a word meaning "old rock."

As believers and the curious weave their way through the narrow streets, they confront the new Lourdes, which grew quickly after finding its niche as a place of pilgrimage. This marriage of the temporal and spiritual Lourdes has produced hotels with names such as Saint-Sacrement, Angélic (not to be confused with the smaller Angélus), Saint Charles, Christ-Roi, Sainte Elisabeth and Saint Sébastien.

Visitors pass store after store selling the same mix of rosaries, medals, postcards, statues, candles and plastic bottles to hold the water from the spring. Many of these stores bear the name of a saint as well as reassurance that credit cards are accepted. The shops of Sainte-Rita, Saint-André, Sainte-Marthe, Sainte-Thérèse and Saint-Mathias, to name just a few, are intermixed with the cafes.

But there is more than all this. The pilgrims walk, wheel or are helped through Saint Joseph's Gate or Saint Michael's Gate to the Sanctuary of Our Lady of Lourdes—or as the enclosed area is known, the Domain. This place seems far removed from modern times. Situated on a parklike campus and bounded on two sides by the River Gave, which serves as a natural divide between the town and the shrine, the Domain invites and welcomes.

The bishop of Tarbes and Lourdes holds authority over the Domain and appoints a rector as his representative. Thirty chaplains representing different congregations, societies and dioceses are permanently assigned to accompany pilgrims, lead prayer and processions and celebrate the sacraments in the more than twenty places of worship. Religious sisters from several communities work in the Sanctuary. A force of approximately 300 full-time employees, more than 100 seasonal workers and thousands of volunteers work together to maintain the shrine and care for visitors.[2]

Passing through Saint Joseph's Gate or Saint Michael's Gate, pilgrims converge at the Statue of the Crowned Virgin. An easily recognizable meeting place for pilgrims, the eight-foot statue of Our Lady rests on an even taller granite pedestal set in the middle of a circular rose garden. Many pilgrims tuck their own flowers into the grillwork of the short fence that surrounds the garden. Erected in 1877, the statue stands vigil at the eastern end of Rosary Square, which can accommodate a crowd of 40,000. On the western end of the square are the Rosary Basilica and, above and behind it, the Basilica of the Immaculate Conception, also known as the upper basilica, which encompasses the Crypt.

Pilgrims crossing Rosary Square at the top of the hour will hear the bells of the upper basilica. The combined bells of Jeanne-Alphonsine (4,400 pounds), Geneviève-Félicie (3,960 pounds), Hermine-Benoîte (2,420 pounds) and their little sister, Cécile-Gastine (1,760 pounds), sing out the *Ave María* of the famous Lourdes hymn ("Immaculate Mary") every hour.

Once they have crossed Rosary Square, pilgrims bear to the right side of the basilicas. They are now just a few steps away from the heart of Lourdes. Unless Mass is being celebrated or the rosary is being recited, prayerful silence signals this new threshold.

Taking a seat on one of the white benches, pilgrims face the very place in which Our Lady appeared to Bernadette eighteen times between February 11 and July 16, 1858. It is the grotto tucked into the side of the rock of Massabielle, which is located opposite the River Gave. What first strikes many pilgrims is that the grotto is a familiar face, a comforting image impressed upon minds and hearts long before they took their first step toward this destination. "It was exactly like the picture I had seen of it," Joan Straka, a wife, mother, grandmother and owner of a popular yarn store, says of her first sight of the grotto.

Not only are pilgrims sure to have seen a photograph or drawing of the grotto, chances run high that they have encountered a grotto "twin." Thousands of replicas of the Grotto of Massabielle grace churches, hospitals, schools and shrines throughout the world.

The rock of Massabielle, which shelters the grotto, is eighty-eight feet high. Small by comparison, the vault of the grotto at its highest point is a little over twelve feet. It is approximately as wide (thirty-two feet) as it is deep (thirty-one feet). Pilgrims' eyes go immediately above the opening to the upper right oval niche in which Mary appeared to Bernadette. Here rests a statue of the Blessed Mother.

The statue of Our Lady of Lourdes reflects—to a limited extent—how the "beautiful girl" appeared to Bernadette. She is dressed in white, the natural finish of the marble, with a blue sash wrapped around her waist. Her rosary beads loop over her hands, folded in prayer. A yellow rose skims each bare foot. At the base of the statue is carved the sculptor's name, Fabisch. Under the base rests the pedestal upon which are the chiseled words in the local dialect that changed forever the destiny of both Bernadette and Lourdes: "*Que soy era Immaculada Concepciou*," "I am the Immaculate Conception."[3]

Two sisters from Lyon commissioned the statue of Mary following a pilgrimage they made to Lourdes in 1863, only five years after the apparitions. The de LaCour sisters wanted to replace a small plaster statue that the people of Lourdes had set in the niche with one hewn from glistening Carrara marble. The sisters intended this new statue to resemble in both size and appearance the apparition that Bernadette saw. Joseph Fabisch, a professor and member of the Academy of Sciences, Arts and Humanities of Lyon, was already well known for his religious art. He personally came to Lourdes with a list of handwritten questions to ask Bernadette about Our Lady's appearance.

Relying on Bernadette's memory and his own artistic instincts, Fabisch fashioned the statue, which was installed on April 4, 1864. From Bernadette's point of view, the statue disappointed. Artistic license had prevailed at the expense of her vision. Fabisch's Our Lady of Lourdes, she confided to Father Peyramale, was too cold, too old and too tall. The artist had disregarded the simplicity of Our Lady both in dress and stance, which Bernadette had described and actually modeled. Instead of portraying Mary with folded hands, palm against palm and fingers pressed together, Fabisch had curved the hands. He also inclined Mary's head, rather than her eyes, toward heaven.

For today's pilgrims, however, this statue, the product of the visionary's recollections and the artist's interpretive hands, draws them closer to the experience of Lourdes. It is the icon recognized immediately by Catholics worldwide as Our Lady of Lourdes.

At eye level and centered in the grotto is the altar, quarried from local stone. It was not the first altar placed here; there have been four others. One of its forerunners can be found in the Lourdes

Grotto in the Vatican Gardens; the local *Musée du Trésor Liturgique* (Liturgical Treasure Museum) houses another.

The stone altar in the grotto reminds pilgrims that Jesus is the rock of our salvation. "The Lord is my rock, and my fortress," the psalmist wrote, "and my deliverer, my God, my rock, in whom I take refuge, my shield, and the horn of my salvation, my stronghold" (Psalm 18:2). Masses have been celebrated daily in the grotto since 1866. Mass is offered in the morning and following the candlelight procession at 11 PM.

There are no barriers to separate visitors from the actual grotto. This was not always the case. The mayor of Lourdes in June 1858 declared the grotto to be off limits for all. At his direction workers erected barricades. The *Lourdais,* collectively proud of both Bernadette and the grotto, tore them down at night. This tango of construction and destruction played out several times before Napoleon III intervened in October 1858 "to liberate the Grotto."[4]

Six years later the clergy installed an iron grill across the front of the grotto, which was opened only when Mass was celebrated. This was to discourage pilgrims from taking rocks and fauna from the site. Visitors had long ago absconded with the bramble bush, the leaves of which Bernadette saw flutter before Our Lady appeared. This grill, with its eight-foot bars, was permanently removed in 1958 for the celebration of the centenary of the apparitions at Lourdes.

Before entering the grotto, pilgrims might notice two plaques on the ground in front of the cave, memorializing two pilgrims who have knelt there. The one directly in front of the altar says, *"ICI, LE 15 AUOT 1983 ET LE 15 AOUT 2004, LE PAPE JEAN-PAUL II EST VENU EN PELERIN"* ("Here, August 15, 1983, and August 15, 2004,

Pope John Paul II came in pilgrimage"). It bears the coat of arms used by John Paul II, with a large "M" for Mary resting under the right side of the cross. The shield on this memorial stone telegraphs visually the late pontiff's devotion to Mary, which his motto, "*Totus Tuus*" ("Totally yours") revealed to the world.

The much smaller plaque, situated to the left of the altar, almost hidden under some benches, recalls the first pilgrim to the grotto, Bernadette. It simply says, "*PLACE OU PRIAT BERNADETTE LE 11 FEVRIER 1858*" ("Place where Bernadette prayed, February 11, 1858").

Now fully aware of the good company they keep, pilgrims are anxious to explore what this small rock shelter holds for them. Entering typically on the left side, they reach out to press their hands against the cold, wet rock of the grotto wall. As they move in clockwise fashion to the back of this recess, they see to the side of the altar—under a clear cover and brightened by a spotlight—the flowing spring that Bernadette unearthed 150 years ago. Today the water is channeled to the taps and the baths.

Pilgrims often pause at the back of the grotto to place their prayer petitions or those they've been carrying for others in the box behind the altar. As they round the inner edge of the grotto, many stop to touch the rock underneath the niche where Mary appeared. The rock face here has been polished smooth by millions of hands throughout the years.

This need to connect—to place one's hand in faith on the rock of Massabielle—affirms for many their belief. For some pilgrims the action shortens the distance between the apparitions and themselves. "Touching it makes us feel that we've been there and we're part of this," according to pilgrim Louise Sutton. The message to Bernadette, Louise notes, was for all ages, including our own.

Tom Joyce said that *not* touching the wall would be unthinkable. The need to touch and to make a connection, he says, is fundamental to what it means to be human. In laying the flat of his palm against the wet, cold rock of the grotto, "that present moment...reaches back and touches the event."

Many pilgrims imagine the grotto in Bernadette's time. The Gave riverbed was closer then; it was pushed back on two occasions between 1858 and 1900 to accommodate the crowds. The slope of the ground under the vault was leveled and a floor constructed. The esplanade between the grotto and the river was enlarged in 1956.

But in 1858 the dark and isolated grotto was chaotic rather than calming. It was a dumping ground, an embarrassment to the community. Wild pigs ran helter-skelter in search of food. Cora Sullivan, having raised five children, shivers slightly when imagining the experience of the fourteen-year-old Bernadette on hearing the wind stir and seeing the soft light in the niche in the grotto. "How frightened she must have been," Cora says.

Franciscan Brother Jim O'Brien admires Bernadette for her fortitude in returning to the grotto. "She had faith. She had belief," he says. "And she continued persistently to come back."

It was in the grotto, against this backdrop of blight where the poorest of the poor scavenged, that the purest of all humankind proclaimed herself to be the Immaculate Conception. The Virgin Mary, her white dress a symbol of purity, stepped into the rock shelter, the messy reserve of the marginalized, the poor and the broken of Lourdes.

Reflecting on the Grotto of Massabielle and Our Lady's appearance there, pilgrims interpret this study in contrasts in different ways. The common threads are humility and love.

Tom Joyce compares Mary's selection of Massabielle with God's selection of Mary to be the mother of our Savior. "Prior to the apparitions, the Grotto of Massabielle was a rugged, seemingly useless crop of rocks that would collect debris and driftwood," he reflects. "It was insignificant, overlooked and assumed to be of little value. The same was true of Mary. She was a Jewish teenage girl, consigned to the backwater, hardscrabble hamlet of Nazareth. She was the antithesis of the power of the age, Rome. Yet when the Lord desired to become man and show his people how to love and to live and to redeem them, whom did he choose? He chose Mary of Nazareth, a handmaid of the Lord." The splendor, power and beauty of the Roman Empire, Tom concludes, could not compare to the beauty of the Immaculate Heart of Mary.

Similarly, "who would have thought that this seemingly useless site would be the foundation of so many conversions, so many changes of heart, so many interior and exterior healings? In short, who would have thought that this rugged Grotto of Massabielle would be the gateway to a smooth, sure path to Christ?" Tom asks.

For Kathleen Gallagher Our Lady's presence in the grotto brings to mind Mary's giving birth to the Son of God in the most humble of surroundings. "I remember sitting there and thinking that there is something about Mary and caves," Kathleen says. "She seems to have an affinity for them. Christ was born in a cave. And here she is appearing in this hull of rock."

Michael McGuire recently graduated from Bucknell University with a double major in political science and Russian and a double minor in linguistics and French. As part of his study-abroad experience, he made a personal weekend pilgrimage to Lourdes. Michael believes that Our Lady chose the Grotto of Massabielle and

Bernadette for a special purpose. He recalls that the locals initially dismissed both as worthless. The conditions of the grotto appeared to him to mirror the poverty of Bernadette and her family, living in the *cachot*. "The grotto is moist, damp, dim, cold and cramped," Michael says, "just like the conditions in which Bernadette lived." The "brilliant, warming presence of Our Lady," he says, intervened in ways unimaginable.

Touching the rock face, contemplating the grotto of more than 150 years ago and offering a prayer—these actions help visitors connect to that point in time when Bernadette hurried to this obscure cave. More importantly, they connect pilgrims to the spoken and unspoken messages that Our Lady conveyed to the young girl. As Mary bore the Son of God in her womb, she carries with her his message of love, which knows no obstacles and overcomes all shortcomings. Our lives, much like the grotto in Bernadette's time, may be disordered, but God nonetheless comes calling. Reaching into the shadows of the caves of our own making, God seeks us through his mother.

As pilgrims replay in their minds the drama that unfolded in the grotto, they detect the seeds of the personal relationship that Mary cultivated with Bernadette, a model for the relationship with God that Our Lady longs her sons and daughters to have. They see the beautiful woman smile at Bernadette, address her with respect and lovingly gaze upon her "as one person looks at another." They hear her politely ask, "Would you do me the kindness of coming here for fifteen days?"

The Virgin's invitation opens for many visitors the floodgates of love. John Botaish, a lawyer and board member for the Denver Lourdes Marian Center, experienced this. Substituting at the last minute for someone unable to make the pilgrimage, John recalls feeling pressed and at loose ends. When he arrived at the grotto, however, he became convinced that Our Lady had intended all along for him to join the pilgrimage. "I felt that I had received a personal invitation from her to be there. I felt her presence there—it was a palpable sensation."

In the intimacy and silence of the grotto, pilgrims bring to the Mother of God all that they are, knowing that she stands ready to intervene on their behalf. "I take my brokenness and the realization that I need God. I take all the things that concern or burden me," Father Clinton Zadroga says of the grotto. "I meet the mother of the Lord there. She and I together at the grotto present all of that to her Son." What he takes away from the grotto, according to Father Clint, is the sense that "I am deeply loved."

Like many pilgrims, Father Michael Walsh of the Denver Lourdes Marian Center brings his faith in God and devotion to Mary to this meeting place of Our Lady and Bernadette. "I go there with faith in the sense that I believe," Father Walsh says. He travels there too with the comforting knowledge that "Mary is able to intercede with her divine Son in heaven for us, for our physical, spiritual or whatever needs we have."

Mary Porter recalls entering the grotto alone, while her father, an Episcopalian priest, and her husband Jeff, an evangelical Protestant, kept their distance. "I had to make that lonely little pilgrimage under their gaze," she remembers.

Mary first encountered Christ through a born-again conversion experience at the age of sixteen, and she asked to be received into the Catholic Church after completing college. Having had little Catholic formation, she straddled for a while the Catholic and

Protestant worlds, serving on nondenominational evangelical mission teams to Haiti, Guatemala and Central Asia and attending Mass when she could.

On a vacation to Spain, Mary routed her family to Fatima and Lourdes. "I wanted my husband and father to experience special graces that could help them come closer to Catholicism," she recalls. She too wanted to draw closer to Mary, about whom she had confidence but also questions. "I was afraid that Mary was someone who stood in the way of Christ, who was stealing glory from Christ rather than bringing him glory," she says.

The trickle of water in the grotto spoke volumes to Mary Porter. "I realized more fully that God chose Mary as the way to bring us closer to Jesus—that God pours out his graces through the instrumentality of the Blessed Virgin Mary and the saints," she explains. In the same place where Mary revealed her identity to Bernadette, Mary Porter embraced it. "Her heart is truly pure. She is the Immaculate Conception, a gift from God. She is full of grace," Mary remembers contemplating.

Unknown to Mary until much later, Jeff was quietly moving beyond the role of spectator at the grotto. He entered the Church in 2004. The Porters named their daughter, now eighteen months old, for her earthly mother and dedicated her to her heavenly one.

Do penance, pray for sinners and come and wash yourself, the Blessed Mother instructed Bernadette as she knelt in the grotto. Pope Benedict XVI, in his Angelus address on February 11, 2007, the Feast of Our Lady of Lourdes and the World Day of the Sick, underscored the importance of that message. "In that place, now almost 150 years ago, the Blessed Mother's call to prayer and penance resounds strongly, almost as a permanent echo of Jesus' invitation which inaugurated his preaching in Galilee: 'The time is fulfilled, and the kingdom of God is at hand; repent, and believe in the Gospel' (Mk 1:15)."[5]

The appearance of the Blessed Virgin and her call for conversion explain the deep affection Sister Anne Marie Gill holds for the grotto. "For me, going into the grotto is going into the embrace of my Mother," Sister Anne Marie says. "I feel so at home there."

Sister Anne Marie belongs to a community founded in 1988, the Franciscan Sisters, Third Order Regular, of Penance of the Sorrowful Mother, whose motherhouse is in Toronto, Ohio. The sisters unite themselves with Mary at the foot of the cross. Through their prayer life of intercession, reparation and atonement, they beg God to open the floodgates of his mercy so that all may be reconciled.

"We actually spend half our time in prayer and half in ministry," Sister Anne Marie explains. As Mary called Bernadette to pray for sinners, these self-described "contemplative penitents committed to works of mercy" feel called to stand in the gap for those who offend God. The religious community joins regularly to praise God, Sister Anne Marie says, "mindful of how Francis encouraged his brothers to praise God in reparation for those who blasphemed God."

While Mary's spoken message resonates with Sister Anne Marie, her unspoken message also finds a home. She is encouraged in recalling that Bernadette reassured her friends that Our Lady, whom they could not see, was smiling at them. "When I go to the grotto, I just imagine Mary smiling with tenderness at me," she says.

The message of Lourdes embraces and compels all, Pope John Paul II said during his final visit in 2004. "From this grotto of Massabielle the Blessed Virgin speaks to us too, the Christians of the third millennium. Let us listen to her!" he urged in his homily on Assumption Day, at a Mass celebrated in the nearby meadow.[6]

"By her words and her silence the Virgin Mary stands before us as a model for our pilgrim way," the pope said. It is not an easy way, he explained, because we suffer the wounds of the sins of our first parents. However, John Paul II encouraged the more than 250,000 pilgrims present and many more spiritually united by radio and television throughout the world, "Evil and death *will not have the last word!* Mary confirms this by her whole life, for she is *a living witness of the victory of Christ, our Passover.*"[7]

For some pilgrims the grotto is best appreciated from a distance. By crossing the River Gave, pilgrims find themselves situated in the very place Bernadette occupied during the final apparition on July 16, 1858. Complying with town ordinances that prohibited visiting the grotto, Bernadette knelt at this distance. The barricades that shuttered the grotto did not prevent her from seeing the Immaculate Conception in all her beauty and warmth.

The view from the other side of the river allows pilgrims to see the grotto in a larger context. Not only do they notice the recess carved out of the bottom of the Rock of Massabielle, but looking up and over the retaining wall, they see fully in side profile the Basilica of the Immaculate Conception, which encompasses the Crypt and from which extends the Rosary Basilica to the front.

"I had seen that church a million times," Tom Joyce says in recalling this surprising discovery. "I had never—until I got on site—made the connection that it was actually built over the grotto."

It is the chapel that Mary requested. The people have come in procession, including Bernadette, who on May 19, 1866, camouflaged in the white uniform of the Children of Mary and hidden in their ranks, marched in the first official procession of Lourdes for the Pentecost weekend dedication of the Crypt. Seeing the grotto from a distance reminds pilgrims of this.

For student Julie Wlotzko, the view of the basilica on top of the grotto reminds her that Mary gives us Christ. She says the challenge is "to pray that our hearts can be made like Mary's, so that we might glorify God by allowing him to rest upon the altar of our hearts. That's symbolized so beautifully in the grotto as the foundation that holds Christ right there." With the wider view from the other side of the Gave, according to Julie, the churches, the grotto and, to the right, the baths speak of all that is essential to Lourdes.

chapter seven

WATER

WHEN BERNADETTE SCRAPED THE GROUND IN THE GROTTO and uncovered the hidden spring on February 25, 1858, she could not have foreseen its immediate and lasting value. "The little spring of Massabielle [is] a living source where faith is renewed, where body and soul are healed and where the sense of the Church is strengthened," Pope John Paul II told the faithful who gathered in Lourdes in 1983.[1]

Today's pilgrims long to respond as Bernadette did to the Blessed Virgin's invitation to "go and drink at the spring and wash yourself there." In imitation of Bernadette's humility and obedience, they too seek this living source of renewal. Deacon Bill Olson of Iowa concisely describes its importance and appeal. "This spring was brought forth by the hand of Bernadette at the direction of Mary, whose presence was willed by God," he explains.

Some years ago the Sanctuary of Lourdes had as its annual pastoral theme, "My soul is thirsting for the living God" (see Psalm 42:2). Bishop Jacques Perrier, bishop of Tarbes and Lourdes, offered pilgrims an approach then that serves equally well today as a guide to navigating the waters of Lourdes. He recommends (1) searching as Bernadette did to discover God's gift for them, (2) washing in the water, (3) drinking at the fountain and (4) sharing the water from the spring, a symbol of God's generosity, with others.[2]

The first step requires listening and responding in faith. Bernadette serves as our instructor. When the Virgin directed her to drink from and wash in the water, her intuitive response was to move toward the familiar and seen—that is, the River Gave directly behind her. But on her way she stopped in her tracks and changed course. Bernadette later explained that the woman in the niche motioned her back to the cave, where no flowing water was in sight. Against all that seemed sensible, she scratched away at the soil, dug deeper and discovered muddy water in the bottom of the hollow.

This Bernadette tried to drink. She spit the muddy water out three times, finally swallowing it on her fourth attempt. She reached into the hole once again and drew out water to "wash" herself. The muddy water smeared on her cheeks made Bernadette look foolish, yet she continued until her aunts dragged her away. Within hours the little spring began to run clear. It continues to this day to provide fresh water.

Bishop Perrier recommends that pilgrims too not reach for what seems to be the "easiest" or the "obvious" path. Like Bernadette, they must be willing to dig below the surface to discover and receive what God wishes to give them.

Washing in the water, the second suggestion offered by the bishop, defines a peak experience of Lourdes for many. Pilgrims today wash in the waters from the same spring that Bernadette did, now channeled to the baths, the taps and the basins of the Water Walk.

The appeal of the Lourdes water is as old as the history of the apparitions themselves. While Our Lady asked Bernadette to drink and wash in the spring, she never promised or even hinted at any healing properties. Before the year's end, however, seven individuals with debilitating health problems who had washed in, applied or drunk the waters of the Massabielle spring were miraculously cured. Over the years the majority of all declared miraculous cures have resulted after the *miraculé* used the spring water.

Pilgrims might wonder what sets this water of Massabielle apart. Routinely subjected to analysis, the water of Massabielle has proven repeatedly to be pure and drinkable but with no curative or therapeutic properties. Its chemical composition mirrors that of other springs in the immediate region.[3]

Lourdes water is not "holy" water, because a priest or deacon has not blessed it liturgically. The water from the grotto may be considered miraculous, however, according to Father René Point, M.I.C., "if what we mean by that is that through the intercession of Mary, God had performed certain miracles in connection with the baths or use of the water from the Grotto." Users of this water, Father Point writes, "must have confidence not in the supposed virtues of the water, but in Mary's 'strength of intercession.'"[4] Bernadette herself said, "You must have faith and pray with perseverance.... This water would have no power without faith."[5]

Water looms large as sign and substance in both the Old and New Testaments. Before there was light, we read in Genesis, "the Spirit of God was moving over the face of the waters" (Genesis 1:2). It is "through the visible creation," according to the *Catechism of the Catholic Church*, that "God speaks to man," and man "can read there traces of its Creator" (1147). In "reading" the waters of the Old

Testament, one sees that our Creator gives life, purifies by destroying that which is evil, satisfies and quenches the thirst of both man and the wilderness, forgives and heals.

In the New Testament Jesus identifies baptism—water and the spirit—as the gateway to the kingdom of God (see John 3:5) and reveals himself as the source of living waters yielding eternal life (John 4:10–14; 7:37–38). In the story of the woman at the well, Jesus promises that "whoever drinks of the water that I shall give him will never thirst; the water that I shall give him will become in him a spring of water welling up to eternal life" (John 4:14).

Father Régis-Marie de La Teyssonnière, Chaplain of Honor of Our Lady of Lourdes, distills beautifully the meaning of the story of the spring of Massabielle. "When Our Lady said to Bernadette, 'Go to the spring to drink and drink from it,' Bernadette finds in the back of the grotto a hidden spring under mud and muddy water. When pure water appears, the grotto itself is washed by that water, and the grotto becomes a place of life, where all are able to receive life."

The scenario played out in the rocky shelter, according to Father de La Teyssonnière, has meaning for our own souls. "The true grotto is our own heart. Being baptized, we have already been washed and have received the spring of water for eternal life. But as mud covered the spring, sins in our heart often hide the spring. And when the spring is hidden, it is difficult to know how to find it." Father de La Teyssonnière suggests that we may even forget that we carry within our hearts "the most incredible treasure, the spring for eternal life!"

Bernadette's pilgrimage, Father de La Teyssonnière reminds us, is not only horizontal but also vertical. "It is symbolic of Jesus' cross. That is the message of Lourdes—reminding us of the gospel," he concludes.

About 350,000 visitors each year choose to bathe in the waters from the spring Bernadette uncovered. They make their way past the grotto and the candle garden to the low-lying building that was constructed in 1955 and upgraded in both 1972 and 1980. Pilgrims see the words of Our Lady inscribed above the entry, "Go Drink at the Spring and Bathe in Its Waters." Separate entrances welcome men and women to the *piscines*. Within the building are seventeen individual baths, with eleven designated for women and six for men. Both the men's and women's sections provide a smaller bath for children.

For first-time bathers the wait on the benches—often long, especially in the summer—can be stressful. Although excited to be there, many cannot help but wonder what lies ahead. The ritual of undressing and stepping into fifty-degree spring water is not something for which the typical twenty-first-century pilgrim has had any preparation or experience.

"I first was very hesitant about doing this. I went up two or three times to ask about it," Louise Sutton says. "Even getting in line made one anxious. Not knowing is always fearful."

It is not only the unknown that makes pilgrims pause. Most are aware that the process requires a stripping away not only of their clothes but of pride and defenses.

Having experienced both bathing in the waters and serving in the baths as a North American Lourdes Volunteer, Julie Wlotzko recognizes the reluctance of pilgrims to bare their bodies—in an ever so modest fashion—and also their souls. "We're all humans. We all need healing—some physical, some spiritual, some emotional," Julie says. "As humans, it's natural to deny that need because you're vulnerable. And vulnerability hurts." The feelings of vulnerability mix with heartfelt prayers and a mental rehearsal of spiritual intentions as pilgrims wait their turn to be admitted to the baths.

The doorkeepers at the separate men's and women's entrances, typically members of the Hospitality of Our Lady of Lourdes, begin their shifts by praying the rosary along with other volunteers. Reflecting the diversity of nationalities who serve, the volunteers pray each decade in a different language. "When we were done praying, we would kiss the floor. I felt that in our prayers, we were really consecrating our shift and the area to Our Lady and for all the women coming through," recalls volunteer Katie Patton.

The doorkeeper summons just a few from the bench at a time. As the recently chosen give up their seats, all the bathers-in-waiting shift positions on the benches, moving steadily closer to the door. Once admitted, pilgrims enter a communal dressing area in which modesty reigns. In the women's section, for example, a volunteer covers the pilgrim with a blue cloak, allowing her to remove her clothes underneath it in privacy. The candidate for bathing then waits to be invited to enter the next section, which is separated by a curtain. When that curtain is pulled back, she crosses the threshold and sits down in a chair.

In front of her and the small number of others waiting within this inner sanctum are a series of side-by-side narrow stalls, each curtained for privacy. From behind those curtains she hears an occasional cry or whimper, when bather and icy water first meet. She hears the movement of the water and soft voices speaking, not necessarily in her native tongue.

Finally a volunteer pulls back the curtain and points to the waiting pilgrim. It is too late to turn back. Her time has arrived to bathe in the waters of the spring.

Stepping into the stall, the bather now stands at the edge of a grey stone tub. At the far end of the tub, a small statue of Our Lady of Lourdes is mounted on the wall. Two volunteers come along either side of the bather; another stands behind. In a swift motion the side helpers wrap and knot a wet towel around the bather, while the volunteer to the rear removes the blue cloak. The bather is never uncovered.

After making the Sign of the Cross and saying a prayer to Our Lady, the bather steps down into the knee-high waters. She then walks the length of the stone tub. The volunteers motion her to sit in the water as if she were in a chair. This is like sitting in the Atlantic Ocean off the New Jersey coast in March.

A volunteer at either side assists the bather in leaning back and immersing herself in the water up to her shoulders. Within a second or two, the volunteers pull her back to her feet. The bather now moves toward and kisses the statue of the Blessed Mother. The volunteers' gentle recitation of prayers fills the stall: "Our Lady of Lourdes, pray for us. Saint Bernadette, pray for us. O Mary, conceived without sin, pray for us who have recourse to thee."

Retracing her steps, the bather wades through the waters and climbs the few steps. The volunteers wrap the blue cloak around her and remove the wet towel. One of the helpers says, "It's out you go," and the bather goes quickly to dress. Lourdes does not provide towels and discourages pilgrims from bringing them to the baths. Within a minute or two of stepping out of the water, the bather is close to dry without toweling off. This is not a consequence of divine intervention but of the quick evaporation resulting from very cold water meeting a warm body.

The scenario is repeated up and down the bathing stalls of the women's section and, in a fairly similar fashion, in the men's section every day of the year in Lourdes.

What pilgrims bring to and take from the waters of Massabielle varies as much as the individual pilgrims. In his final pilgrimage to Lourdes in 2004, Pope John Paul II revisited the meaning of the spring. Its waters, the pope said, signify the new life that Christ gives to all who turn to him. And just as the Blessed Virgin asked Bernadette to humble herself in the grotto, John Paul II explained, Mary invites all to this spring of new life, asking them "to renounce their pride and to learn humility so that they can draw from the mercy of her Son and thus work together for the dawn of the civilization of love."[6]

This was to a large extent how Father Clinton Zadroga sized up his experience of going into the waters on three separate pilgrimages. "I see it as an act of humility," he says. "There is a sense of laying aside any illusion of self-sufficiency and coming face-to-face with the fact that I am in need of the gift of God's love. That's what's renewing."

Going into the waters also speaks to many pilgrims of cleansing, purifying and experiencing new life. Just as Bernadette scraped at the mud in the grotto to uncover the spring, pilgrims seek to scrape and wash away the mud in their lives—the sins that prevent them from loving God and their neighbor. This longing to change, to reject sin and turn toward God, describes the intent of baptism, "the principal place for the first and fundamental conversion" (CCC, 1427). Going into the waters helps pilgrims consciously relive their baptism and recall the grace of that moment. Many pilgrims receive the sacrament of reconciliation before or after bathing in the waters of Lourdes, bringing this experience of symbolic conversion to actual completion.

Louise Sutton, who was at first hesitant to go into the baths, remembers, "The submerging reminded me of baptism. It was another indication of God's mercy and our need to reflect on always being cleansed interiorly." The spring that flowed through the baths, Louise says, encouraged her to plumb the depths of her own soul and ask, "Is there an opening within my own being, within my own soul, within my own heart, of a wellspring that results in a greater love for God?"

Tom Joyce said that for him, going into the waters was a deliberate choice to revisit his baptism. "Here I am. I am forty-one. I have a chance to be recollected and say, yes, I want to do this. This is my saying, in miniature, yes to my baptism. I went into the baths fully cognizant of what that meant, fully knowing what that entailed." Tom brought to the experience his gratitude for all that God has given to him and contrition for his shortcomings.

Our Lady's urging to go to the waters and wash, Tom said, was for him a reprise of the sacraments of both baptism and penance. When bathing in the waters is viewed within the context of all that Lourdes offers, including penance and Holy Eucharist, Tom continues, pilgrims realize that "it's an all-encounter with Christ. It's all about him."

Going into the baths symbolizes baptism and more for Franciscan Brother Jim O'Brien. As staff nurse for the U.S. National Rosary Pilgrimage, Brother Jim works to ensure that individuals with special health needs who wish to bathe at Lourdes have that opportunity.

He encourages reluctant pilgrims to consider water in a broad sense.

"Think of the significance of water in our lives. As babies *in utero*, we're floating in water. As birth is coming, the waters break and we come forth. Then, what are we baptized with? Water. When we die, we are blessed with holy water. Water plays such a role in our lives."

On the shady right bank of the River Gave, opposite the grotto, pilgrims find another way to wash in the waters of the spring. The Water Walk consists of nine "points" of water. Each point is actually a wide, round, permanent silver dispenser, about shoulder high, that channels the water of the spring of Massabielle through a tap. A drawing on all the dispensers illustrates that the water from these taps is for washing or for splashing on one's face, not for drinking or to carry home.

Pilgrims are invited, individually or as a group, to visit the points of water. Some groups elect to renew their baptismal vows within a liturgical service conducted along the Water Walk. Others simply visit each point of water, perhaps pausing at one to wash. The points along the Water Walk are easily accessible to all pilgrims, including those in wheelchairs.

Each water point is named for a well or other source of water in the Bible, coupled with at least one title for the Blessed Mother. One, for example, commemorates the well of Beersheba, where Abraham established a covenant with Abimelech. This peace-making agreement assured Abraham, a sojourner, of both well and water rights in a land he did not possess (see Genesis 21:25–34).

Abraham was no stranger to covenants. "God chose Abraham and made a covenant with him and his descendants," states the *Catechism of the Catholic Church*. "By the covenant God formed his people and revealed his law to them through Moses. Through the prophets, he prepared them to accept the salvation destined for all humanity" (72).

At this water point pilgrims invoke the intercession of Our Lady, the Ark of the New Covenant. They remember that Our Lady carried in her womb the Word incarnate, from whose heart water and blood would flow for us (see John 19:33–37).

Another stop along the Water Walk recalls the road to Gaza, along which the apostle Philip proclaimed the good news of Christ to the eunuch. After Philip instructed him, they came upon some water. Philip went down into it with the eunuch and baptized him (see Acts 8:26–39). At this point of water, pilgrims remember Bernadette's "catechist," Mary, Mother of Good Counsel.

Just a few steps away are the points of water representing Meribah (see Exodus 17:1–7), where the Israelites hardened their hearts and tested the Lord (aligned with Our Lady of Sorrows); the springs of En-Gedi (see Song of Solomon 1:13–14), the largest oasis on the western shore of the Dead Sea (Our Lady of Joy); and the spring of the new temple promised by the prophet Ezekiel (see Ezekiel 47:1–12). This latter spring is none other than Christ, "the living water" (see John 7:37–39), who saves all peoples. It is aligned with Our Lady of Fatima or Guadalupe, Our Lady of Czestochowa or Vailankanni and Queen of the Apostles.

Rounding out the remaining stops on this scriptural Water Walk are the springs of Nazareth (see Luke 2:51–52) and Our Lady of the Beatitudes; Jacob's well (see John 4:1–26) and Our Lady of the Living Water; the pool of Bethesda (see John 5:1–18) and Our Lady of Salvation; and the pool of Siloam (see John 9) and Our Lady of the Light.[7]

The Blessed Virgin prescribed to Bernadette not only washing in the waters but also drinking from the spring. This is the third way in which Bishop Perrier suggests pilgrims encounter the water of Massabielle.

Facing the grotto, pilgrims find to its left along the wall various taps yielding water from the spring. Day and night visitors cup their hands under the taps or fill bottles from which to drink. The water is free to anyone who wants it. The pure, cold spring water refreshes. It should also prompt us to pray, Bishop Perrier says, "for those people who are thirsty and that we may always be thirsty for living water."[8]

More than one-sixth of the human family lacks access to clean water,[9] yet there is another thirst that is equal to or even greater than physical thirst. "So many people are living in the desert. And there are so many kinds of deserts," Benedict XVI said in his homily during the Mass in which he was inaugurated as pontiff. The world, the pope says, encompasses the deserts of poverty, hunger, abandonment, loneliness, destroyed love and "the emptiness of souls no longer aware of their dignity or the goal of human life." According to the Holy Father, "The external deserts in the world are growing, because the internal deserts have become so vast."[10]

Concluding his first letter to the Church, *God Is Love*, the pope invoked Mary's help to lead us to Jesus, so that we might be fountains of living water amid the deserts of today's world:

Holy Mary, Mother of God,
you have given the world its true light,
Jesus, your Son—the Son of God.
You abandoned yourself completely

to God's call
and thus became a wellspring
of the goodness which flows forth from him.
Show us Jesus. Lead us to him.
Teach us to know and love him,
so that we too can become
capable of true love
and be fountains of living water
in the midst of a thirsting world.[11]

Taking home water for one's own use and sharing it with others, the fourth encounter recommended by Bishop Perrier, extends the blessings of Lourdes. Because the Sanctuary of Lourdes sells no containers, the pilgrims find themselves returning to the stores they might have bypassed earlier. The breadth of choice in size, shape, design and price amazes and sometimes amuses.

Many pilgrims carry containers that can be tucked in a pocket or attached to a strap and worn over the shoulder. The heartiest can be seen lugging five-liter containers. While most of the plastic containers are rectangular, some conform to the shape of the grotto or the figure of the "beautiful lady." Images of the grotto, the Virgin and Bernadette are stamped in blue ink on many of these containers-to-go.

What prompts pilgrims to carry water home from Lourdes? It weighs them down, spills if it's not tightly capped and often must be stashed in checked luggage because of airport security regulations. Nonetheless, millions of pilgrims take with them not only their memories of Lourdes but also water from the spring. They earmark this remembrance for family, friends, coworkers and their parishes, which may use it for healing services and visits to the sick.

The pilgrims recognize that the water they carry home is a living sign of the healing and renewing presence of God's love made real through Mary.

Katie and Karl Orbon packed water from the grotto in their bags. "We brought it back because people have been cured through and with the help of Lourdes water," Katie explains. "People asked us to bring back Lourdes water. You want to have it on hand if somebody needs it."

Karl Orbon figures the water provides an easy way to reach out to people who do not share their Catholic faith. People appreciate the gesture even if they don't have a theological understanding of Mary or believe that miracles have taken place at Lourdes. "It's a good bridge to people to say that we went and prayed where we believe Our Lady appeared. 'We asked the Blessed Mother to look after you and your family, and we brought you this water,'" Karl says. "They appreciate the fact that you would do that."

For pilgrims who are unable to carry water home and for people who have not been fortunate enough to visit the shrine, the Sanctuary of Our Lady of Lourdes offers the spring water at no cost to individuals throughout the world. There is a charge, however, for the container, handling and shipping, which can be costly depending on the requestor's place of residence. The *Service expédition d'eau* also ships large containers across the Atlantic to three places in North America currently authorized to distribute it: the original Lourdes Center in Boston, the Lourdes Marian Center in Denver and the Shrine of St. Bernadette in Albuquerque, New Mexico.

The Lourdes Center in Boston, founded by the late Archbishop Cardinal Richard Cushing, opened its doors in 1950 and received its first shipment of water in January 1951. Since that time, according to the current director, Father Martin Normand, S.M., the center has shipped countless containers of water throughout North America. The Marist Fathers and Brothers, who trace their congregational roots to France, have from the start ministered at the center.

Archbishop Charles Chaput blessed and officially dedicated the Denver Lourdes Marian Center on January 1, 2003, with Bishop Jacques Perrier of the diocese of Tarbes and Lourdes and Father Patrick Jacquin, then rector of the Sanctuary of Our Lady of Lourdes, in attendance. The center's founder and spiritual director, Father Michael Walsh, guides the site, which opened on February 11, 2002, the Feast of Our Lady of Lourdes, and is staffed by volunteers.

Both Lourdes centers—east and west—ship water in pocket-sized plastic containers, requesting a small contribution to defray shipping costs. Promoting devotion to Our Lady and making known the message of Lourdes are the goals of both centers, in addition to distributing water from the spring.

John Botaish serves as the president of the board for Denver's Lourdes Marian Center. He credits the Blessed Mother with being its "best ambassador," as measured by the thousands of requests they receive for water from people coast to coast. While requests come mostly from Catholics, people of other faith traditions also ask for the water from the grotto. This water gives hope, and that hope, the center's Father Walsh explains, rests in God, using the water as a means for healing.

The Shrine of St. Bernadette began as St. Bernadette Church in Albuquerque. Archbishop Michael J. Sheehan, archbishop of Santa Fe, raised it to a shrine in 2003. The shrine encompasses the Bernadette Chapel. There one can see a bronze replica of Saint

Bernadette's incorrupt body, which resides in the motherhouse chapel of the Sisters of Charity of Nevers, France. A museum documents Bernadette's life through photos, relics and artifacts of the saint. Our Lady of Lourdes Grotto contains a pool at its base, containing water from the spring. The shrine offers Lourdes water to visitors and also ships it to those who request it.

Chapter Eight

. • .

L I G H T

A TOWER OF TALL CANDLES BURNS BRIGHTLY DAY AND NIGHT
in front of the Grotto of Massabielle, always in shade given its
northern face. The large iron candelabrum, with its six circles of
tapers stacked in wedding-cake fashion, is topped by a single candle
in the center, the burning flame of which dances not far from the
base of the hollow in which Our Lady first appeared to Bernadette.

It was in this niche of the rock of Massabielle that Bernadette
first saw the brambles stir and then the gentle light appear in the
shadowy recess. And within that light she glimpsed the beautiful girl
who beckoned to her. Both the light and the Lady dressed in white
would be for Bernadette's eyes only. The many others who witnessed the later apparitions saw only the shining face of Bernadette,
with her eyes fixed on the dark cavity of the rock. Her transfigured
face reflected the light and goodness of the Virgin.

The candles burn today in the grotto as reminders of the light
that accompanied Our Lady's presence and of Bernadette, who
more times than not carried a borrowed candle with her. Memories

linger here too of the "miracle of the candle," the time when the flames of a candle licked repeatedly at the hands of Bernadette in ecstasy but left neither blister, mark nor memory.

While the candles bear testimony to the Blessed Mother and Bernadette, on another level they symbolize pilgrims' search for the inner light—the light of faith, the light of the world. "I am the light of the world," Jesus said. "Whoever follows me will never walk in darkness but will have the light of life" (John 8:12, NRSV).

Since 1872 pilgrims have carried candles in procession at Lourdes. On a late summer evening of that year, Father Marie-Antoine, a Capuchin, watched as flickering candles placed in the grotto kept company with a small group of pilgrims who remained to pray. "All these candles must walk and sing!" he thought.[1] He invited the pilgrims to sing *Ave Maria Stella* in front of the grotto. The next night hundreds more joined in the singing as they carried candles.

At the height of pilgrimage season in Lourdes today, tens of thousands of men, women and children continue the tradition. Each holds a candle and processes through the Domain praying, singing and celebrating the Son of God. The candles remind them of their baptism, the sacrament in which they were "enlightened" by receiving the Word and became children of the light and, in fact, "light" itself (see CCC, 1216).

Between April and mid-October, pilgrims start to assemble in the grotto around 8:30 PM for the candlelight Marian procession. Each pilgrimage group carries a banner or flag identifying who they are and from where they hail. They bring with them the slender white candles and companion paper lanterns that they have purchased in town. The lanterns, which are used to shield the flame from the wind, have four sides imprinted with hymns to Mary in the pilgrims' language of choice, with one panel frequently reserved for the Latin hymn *Salve Regina*.

Pilgrims with special needs wait patiently in their blue *voitures*. Assisted by the volunteers of Our Lady of Lourdes Hospitality, the sick will enjoy pride of place as the leaders of this procession.

In his final visit to Lourdes in 2004, the ailing John Paul II himself stayed at the Accueil Notre-Dame, and from there he introduced the candlelight procession. The pontiff's words that night paid homage to both Mary and her Son. "This year the Pope joins you in this act of devotion and love for the Most Holy Virgin, the glorious woman of the Book of Revelation, crowned with twelve stars," he said. "Holding in our hands *the lighted torch,* we recall and profess our faith in the Risen Christ. *From him the whole of our life receives light and hope.*"[2]

When the journey of light and hope is about to begin, the bearers of the statue of Our Lady of Lourdes slip into place in front of the sick. The illuminated statue is a resin model of the larger statue, sculpted by Cabuchet, found today in the Basilica of the Immaculate Conception. Pilgrims holding torches step alongside the statue bearers to escort Our Lady.

A different pilgrimage group leads the procession each evening. Elizabeth Grinder, executive director of the U.S. National Rosary Pilgrimage, recalls what a privilege this is. "We've been fortunate enough to have been given the honor of leading some of the night processions," she says. "Men of the pilgrimage will carry the crowned Virgin statue, and our priests will lead."

A few minutes before the start, the chaplain of the Sanctuary, speaking in French, welcomes the pilgrims, identifies the groups present and announces the evening's prayer intentions. This is then repeated in English, Italian, Dutch, German and Spanish—the other official languages of the Domain.

As the bells ring out from the upper basilica at 9 PM, the chaplain leads the pilgrims in making the Sign of the Cross, signaling the start of the favorite prayer of Bernadette, the rosary. Bernadette prayed the rosary at the beginning of each appointment she kept with the "beautiful lady" at the grotto.

Simple but profound, the rosary has been described by Pope Benedict XVI as the "prayer of the Christian who advances on his pilgrimage of faith."[3] In Mary's company the pilgrims contemplate the face of Christ in his incarnation and hidden years (the Joyful Mysteries), his public life (the Luminous Mysteries), his passion and death (the Sorrowful Mysteries) and his triumph over death (the Glorious Mysteries). In reflecting on these mysteries, Pope John Paul II urged believers to imitate Mary at the Annunciation and "to ask humbly the questions which open us to the light, in order to end with the obedience of faith: 'Behold I am the handmaid of the Lord; be it done to me according to your word' (Lk 1:38)."[4]

Each mystery of the rosary is announced along with a biblical meditation. The pilgrim choir, an assembly of volunteers from all over the world, sings a canticle to the Virgin. The pilgrims then pray the Our Father in Latin, followed by the first decade of the rosary. The first five Hail Marys are prayed in one language, the next five in another throughout the evening. All join in chanting in Latin the Glory Be and in singing the refrain of "Immaculate Mary."

The pilgrims are on the move now. Leaving the grotto, they follow the Esplanade, the oval walkway through the Domain. As one decade of the rosary gives way to another, the pilgrims join in singing the common refrain, *Ave, Ave, Ave, María*. With each *Ave* they lift higher the candles they hold.

Light overcomes darkness and diminishes differences. We see in this moment the universality of the Church. Many pilgrims speak of the strong unspoken bond among the people of many nations processing in these streams of light. John Paul II observed this at Lourdes in 1983. "We pray, no longer silently but as a great number following the Risen Christ. We enlighten each other. We carry each other along. We depend on our faith in Jesus, on his words which are a light for our hearts," the pope encouraged. "Jesus tells us: 'Keep your lamps lit!'—the light of Faith, the light of prayer. May our prayers unite and ascend towards God, like the flames of our candles."[5]

Marlene Watkins, president of North American Lourdes Volunteers, refers to this "aha moment" as the instant that crowns in faith the young people she brings to Lourdes. "One of the youth always figures it out," Marlene says. "They say, 'You know what? It's really true. It's here. We're in it.'" The "it" to which she is referring is the Church catholic, the *universal* Church. According to Marlene, witnessing "thirty thousand people all praying the rosary and all in their own languages—Arabic, Chaldean, German, Gaelic, Korean, Zulu and every other language" confirms the universality of the Church for the high school and college volunteers. "You would think it would be like the Tower of Babel," she said, "but it's not. It's Pentecost!"

It's not just the youth who are confirmed in their sense of Church and of faith by the participation in the torchlight procession. Kathleen Gallagher, who on one pilgrimage spent a night watching the procession and another night marching in it, said,

"When you look down and see the thousands of people there with their torches of light saying the rosary in different languages and singing the Lourdes hymn, tears come to your eyes, because it is like the whole Church in unity in front of you."

Louise Sutton recalled a similar experience. "You see these thousands and thousands of people carrying candles and saying the rosary. These people were praying in their own language but all in tune with the same purpose of why they were there honoring the Mother of God," she said. "All nationalities, all colors, all countries, are coming here to inwardly enhance their belief and their love for the Mother of God as our advocate. That indeed is what she is. Her message to us is that we honor and love her Son, but she is always there as an advocate for us to plead our cause, to intercede for us and to watch over us." Louise believes the experience gives a foretaste for the end of time, when all will be united as one in their praise and love of God.

Brother Jim O'Brien, O.F.M. CONV., was eighteen years old when he participated in his first candlelight procession. Now, after more than two dozen pilgrimages to Lourdes, the procession, or as he describes it, "the winding way of light," still stirs his soul. "In all the darkness of our pain and our sorrow, there is a glimmer of hope, there is a glimmer of light," he says. "We're all praying. There is such a sense of family and camaraderie. We're all from different countries. We all speak different languages. You're shoulder-to-shoulder and neck-to-neck with people. Even though they can't verbally speak your language, the language of love comes through very clearly."

In spite of differences in nationality and language, Joan Straka remembers that "everyone was on the same mission, the same journey." At Lourdes, she says, "we are all part of a huge, huge family—a part of this mystical body of Christ." In the candlelight procession, Father Michael Walsh of the Denver Lourdes Marian Center agrees, the universality of the Church is made visible. "You see people from every tribe and every nation," he says, "It is a picture of the experience of the Church worldwide."

Many find the candlelight procession to be an experience like no other. "When I am at Lourdes, I do what all pilgrims do," Father Régis-Marie de la Teyssonnière, Chaplain of Honor of Our Lady of Lourdes, recounts, "but I especially love doing what I am not able to do in other places. I love to attend the candlelight procession, being hidden among twenty or thirty thousand or more. It is for me a great privilege to be one of the people of God."

As the procession approaches the Rosary Basilica, participants wind in one direction, cross the square and then wind in the opposite direction, all the while moving forward. As seen from the ramps reaching to the upper basilica, the pilgrims appear to be ribbons of light continually advancing until the whole square is filled. Now facing the front of the lighted basilica, all sing the *Salve Regina* and, for the final time, lift high their candles in praise. The bells of the Basilica of the Immaculate Conception ring out. The bishops and priests bless the sick at the front of the crowd and give their final blessing to all. Everyone extends to his or her neighbor a sign of peace.

While the procession has come to a close, a blazing fire burns in an elevated basin in front of the Rosary Basilica. It reminds pilgrims of the fire from which the paschal candle is lit during the Service of Light of the Easter Vigil. This candle represents the "light of Christ, rising in glory" and dispelling "the darkness of our hearts and minds."[6]

The crowd slowly disperses, content in the knowledge that Mary's request has once again been fulfilled: "Go and tell the priests that people should come here in procession." Many head back to the cafes or hotels to relax and share with others the memories of the day. Some stay for the Mass in the grotto, which begins at 11:00 PM. This last Mass, celebrated in French four nights a week and in Italian the remaining nights, is offered in thanksgiving for all the graces received that day in the Sanctuary. Exposition of the Blessed Sacrament follows Mass, a poignant "mother and Son" reunion in which our Lord is adored in the very place where his mother has been honored throughout the day.

Other pilgrims, alone or with family members or friends, quietly make their way past the grotto to the *brûloirs*, the metal racks holding a thousand candles of different sizes. Above the racks on the back wall is written, "This flame continues my prayer."

"I remember standing there at night," Katie Orbon recalls. "You are surrounded by all the candles. You can feel the heat of it. You're tangibly seeing somebody else's prayers. You're adding yours. It is so beautiful to see them all together, to see the smoke of hope rising up."

Pilgrims throughout the day and late into the night place their candles here. No fewer than 750 tons of candles burn brightly in the *brûloirs* each year. The flames of the individual candles die out in about two or three hours.[7] Less easily measured are the intentions of the heart that accompany them. In the silence of the burning flames, how many pilgrims have whispered prayers begging Mary to intercede with her Son for a deepening of faith, restoration of health, reuniting of family, the blessing of a baby, the dignity of work or a happy death? How many have come here to give thanks for a grace granted, a bullet dodged or a hope renewed? For this there is no measure.

The light that pilgrims seek in Lourdes is found beyond the grotto, beyond the "walking candles" of the procession and beyond the *brûloirs*. The light of the sacraments, Sister Anne Marie Gill says, draws pilgrims. "There's such a permeation of God's grace. The sacraments are everywhere. Everything centers around the sacraments."

In preparing for the sacrament of penance, which is readily available at Lourdes, pilgrims seek the light to see themselves as they truly are. Much like Bartimaeus, the blind man of Jericho, they beg, "Lord, that I may see" (see Mark 10:51). In examining their consciences, they ask God to give light to their souls so that they may realize the areas of darkness in which they live. "With the sacrament of penance—if you honestly approach it—light can be shed into your heart to see the areas in which you can grow and change," Tom Joyce says.

The fruit of this exercise in self-knowledge and interior repentance, according to the *Catechism of the Catholic Church*, is nothing less than the "radical reorientation of our whole life" (1431)—a conversion in which we turn our hearts toward God, turn our backs on sin and resolve to begin anew with the help of God's grace and mercy. Is it any wonder that so many pilgrims make their way to the Chapel of Reconciliation while at Lourdes?

A statue of Saint John Vianney, the Curé of Ars, kneeling in prayer marks the spot of the Chapel of Reconciliation, located to the right of Rosary Square along the riverbank. Saint John Vianney (1786–1859), who struggled with his studies to become a priest, enjoys to this day the reputation of confessor *par excellence*. Living humbly, poorly and prayerfully, he spent more than fifteen hours a day in the confessional during the last ten years of his life. His renown as a spiritual director and "reader of souls" drew thousands of penitents to his small village northwest of Lyon, France.

In the spirit of Saint John Vianney, the chaplains of the Sanctuary invite pilgrims to confess their sins and to be reconciled with God and the Church. The brightly lit chapel houses forty-eight confessionals and an area for reflection. On the ground floor priests hear confessions in English, French, Spanish, German and Dutch; on the floor above priests administer the sacrament in Italian and Polish.

There is no shortage of penitents in Lourdes, nor reasons for wanting to receive the sacrament there. In this sacrament of healing, pilgrims embrace in a life-changing way what they enact in the baths and on the Water Walk. In washing in the waters of the spring, many recall their baptism, the sacrament in which they first encountered the light of salvation and removal of sin. In confessing and receiving absolution, penitents reignite not symbolically but in actuality the spark of the divine within them. "For once you were darkness, but now you are light in the Lord," Saint Paul writes, "walk as children of light" (Ephesians 5:8). The pilgrims leave the Chapel of Reconciliation enlightened for the road ahead.

Father Clinton Zadroga views the experience of washing in the waters and receiving the sacrament of penance as inseparable. Father Clint witnessed firsthand the enthusiasm for receiving the sacrament when he last visited Lourdes. As he prepared to make his own confession in the chapel, he noticed a long line of students from Seton Hall University in New Jersey. Eventually one of the students asked him if he spoke English and, learning that he did, inquired if he might be able to help.

After confessing and then obtaining permission from the resident English-speaking chaplain, Father Clint heard many of the students' confessions. In reflecting on that time, he says that celebrating penance in the context of a pilgrimage is a special grace. People have come many miles and have spent the journey preparing themselves for all that they might experience at a sacred place. "God blesses that and allows the celebration of the sacrament of penance to be more intense," according to Father Clint. "I think the pilgrimage creates in us a better disposition for the experience of conversion."

Many pilgrims who receive the sacrament of penance at Lourdes do so in response to Our Lady's personal call for conversion. "Penance, penance, penance," she told Bernadette. It may also be the distance from home and the anonymity of confessing to a stranger that encourage many to seek God's mercy at the Chapel of Reconciliation. Cora Sullivan appreciates how the confessors were "very helpful and very human and made you feel totally at ease with anything in your life you were worried about." Thinking about the many pilgrims who pass through the Chapel of Reconciliation, Cora smiles and says, "The priests who are there have heard it all!"

The chapel used to be located at the foot of the Way of the Cross. While no longer physically proximate, both the Chapel of Reconciliation and the Way of the Cross share the common intersection of conversion. "The human heart is converted by looking upon him whom our sins have pierced," the Catechism instructs (1432).

The Way of the Cross at Lourdes represents a pilgrimage within a pilgrimage. Those who scale the nearly mile-long path on the steep

Espélugues Hill, accessed near the Basilica of the Immaculate Conception, journey with Christ on the road to Calvary. They walk the sad route with him, on which he is condemned, carries his cross and falls under its weight. They meet those individuals of light, Simon of Cyrene and Veronica, who step out of the shadows to help. They witness the heartache of the mother as she encounters her Son.

At the summit of the hill sunlight streams, and pilgrims stand or kneel as they see the crucified Son of God. As they walk down the hill, they see the tomb in which he is laid.

One-hundred-fifteen larger-than-life cast-iron figures, each bronzed, make up the tableau of the original fourteen stations. Constructed by Maison Raffi of Paris, the Way of the Cross was developed in the early 1900s, made possible through the generosity of several pilgrimage groups. A fifteenth station, the Resurrection, a large circle of stone with carved rays of light emanating from the center, was added later to remind pilgrims that the cross and the Resurrection are one movement of Jesus toward the Father.

While reflections may vary, a booklet offered by the Sanctuary encourages pilgrims to meditate on the sufferings of Jesus depicted at each station and then to consider Bernadette in light of that experience. For example, at the tenth station, "Jesus is stripped of his garments," those making the Way of the Cross are reminded that "Bernadette humiliated herself by kissing the ground, eating grass and washing her face in the muddy water. But she then allowed God to clothe her in his love, a love she lived the rest of her life."[8]

Karen Landau, wife and mother of two sons, made the Way of the Cross several times on her pilgrimage to Lourdes. It attracted her as a means of meditating on the suffering of Christ as well as on the suffering of the many pilgrims who come to Lourdes.

"Jesus asked us to follow the Way. He asked us to endure our sufferings with patience and to be in union with him in our sufferings," Karen says. She was struck not only by the people with special needs who made their way up the hill but also by those who assisted them. "I had to sit down because I was overtaken by awe," she says in considering the sacrifices of those who came alongside the physically challenged. "They were doing this because their hearts were so deeply troubled for the suffering of the other one."

More accessible Stations of the Cross are located outdoors along the River Gave; and in the underground Basilica of St. Pius X, the stations are presented in glass. Lourdes will unveil in 2008 a new Way of the Cross sculpted by Maria de Faykod in Carrara marble. They will include fifteenth (Holy Saturday) and sixteenth (the Resurrection) stations and will be located on the prairie, near the Tent of Adoration.

No greater light can be found at Lourdes than the light of Christ in the Eucharist. "This Eucharist is a mystery of light!" John Paul II proclaimed at the start of the Year of the Eucharist in 2003. While Christ's divine glory radiates in the Transfiguration and Resurrection, it remains veiled in the Eucharist. "Through the mystery of his complete hiddenness, Christ becomes a mystery of light, thanks to which believers are led into the depths of the divine life,"[9] John Paul II wrote. In receiving Jesus in the Eucharist, the faithful "pass from the light of the Word to the light streaming from the 'Bread of life,' the supreme fulfillment of his promise to 'be with us always, to the end of the age' (cf. Mt 28:20)."[10]

Bernadette's deep longing for the Eucharist compelled her to leave Bartrès and her work as a shepherdess and return to Lourdes. Her arrival home took place within three weeks of the first apparition. Shortly after that apparition she made her first confession. On June 3, 1858, about two weeks before the final apparition, Bernadette received her first Holy Communion from the hand of Father Peyramale.

Pilgrims today, like Bernadette, are called to adore and receive the Eucharist. In more than fifty Masses celebrated daily in the grotto, the Crypt, the basilicas, the churches and the chapels of this Marian shrine, pilgrims have this privilege. "The Virgin Mary shows me here that as amazing as her love is and as beautiful a gift as the apparitions are to the Church," Father Clinton Zadroga says, "these gifts pale in comparison to the gift of the Eucharist. I feel at Lourdes too a greater awareness that Our Lady is worshiping with us."

In knowing that "the Lord is still with us, our faithful companion along the way," Benedict XVI writes, we experience true joy.[11] Since the centenary celebration of the apparitions in 1958, a religious community, the Daughters of the Church, have experienced the joy of quiet companionship with Jesus through their apostolate of adoration at Lourdes. Depending on the time of day and the season, pilgrims may also adore and worship Jesus in the Blessed Sacrament in the Tent of Adoration, the Adoration Chapel or the Crypt.

chapter nine

Wheat

Pilgrims must eventually leave Lourdes, just as did Bernadette. On July 3, 1866, she prayed at the grotto, her "heaven on earth," for the last time before joining her family for a farewell meal. The twenty-two-year-old Bernadette bid loved ones good-bye the next morning as she stepped into the coach that would take her from the hospice school of Lourdes to the train station. Her Aunt Basile would later recall that everyone cried but Bernadette. "How good of you to cry," her aunt remembered Bernadette saying, "but I can't stay here forever."[1]

Bernadette had set her sights on becoming a member of the Sisters of Charity and Christian Instruction. In the company of two sisters and two other postulants—including Léotine Mouret, also from the hospice—she reached St. Gildard Convent, the order's motherhouse in Nevers, on July 7 at 10:30 PM. It was probably too late for Bernadette to notice the motto of the sisters etched into the building, *Deus Caritas Est* (God is Love), a motto she would later make her own.

At the insistence of her superiors, the next day Bernadette stood in front of the curious sisters. Clothed for the last time in her blue peasant dress and white hood, she told her story of the visitations of the Blessed Virgin and her own calling to become a nun. With that behind her, Bernadette put on the pleated cap and cape of the postulant and gratefully stepped into the anonymity of religious life.

"I came to hide myself," Bernadette explained.[2] Rejecting any special attention, she later would compare herself to a broom used by the Virgin Mary. "What do you do with a broom when you have finished using it?" Bernadette asked. "You put it away behind the door. That's my place and that's where I'm staying."[3]

Homesickness visited Bernadette quickly, as it did other postulants. She wrote good-naturedly to the sisters at the Lourdes hospice that she and Léotine "gave a good watering to the whole of Sunday with our tears." She missed, of course, her family and the mountains. In the same letter Bernadette revealed, however, another yearning. She asked the sisters to remember her when they went to the grotto. "That is where you will find me in spirit, *clinging to the foot of that ledge I love so much*," she wrote just two weeks after arriving in Nevers.[4]

Before the month ended, Bishop Forcade faced the group of postulants, each clothed in the habit of the community with a bridal veil loosely covering her head. Reminding the young women that they had chosen Jesus Christ as their spouse, the bishop replaced the bridal veil with a black one. From this day forward Bernadette, now a novice, would be known as Sister Marie-Bernard, a slight twist to the name given to her in baptism.

The new Sister Marie-Bernard watched as one novice after another was dispatched to the community's ministries throughout France to complete formation. Her superiors thought it wise to shield her from curious outsiders. Her mission field as a novice and for the rest of her years as a professed sister would be within the walls of St. Gildard Convent.

Bernadette's health, always fragile, worsened quickly at Nevers. Anticipating her death, the sisters called upon the bishop on October 25, 1866, to administer the sacrament of extreme unction and to receive her vows. Too weak to pronounce the words of commitment, Sister Marie-Bernard said "Amen" to the promises that the bishop read. She recovered, much to the surprise of many, including her superior. "They can't send me away," an amused Sister Marie-Bernard later said.

On October 30, 1867, Sister Marie-Bernard, in the company of the novices with whom she had trained, restated her intention to live in poverty, chastity, obedience and, in keeping with her religious community, charity. Once again her companions—now professed sisters—were given "obediences" at the houses staffed by the Sisters of Charity. After dismissing Sister Marie-Bernard as "good for nothing," the superior, in a practiced exchange with the bishop directed at keeping the young sister in her humble state, admitted that Sister Marie-Bernard might be somewhat suited to help in the infirmary, since she was always sick. Turning to Sister Marie-Bernard, the bishop assigned her the job of prayer.

Sister Marie-Bernard embraced both missions. A practical, calm young woman who had cared for family members and assisted the elderly at the hospice, Sister Marie-Bernard found a niche in the infirmary. She encouraged the sick as well as the other sisters through her love, joyfulness and frankness. As the years passed, however, the infirmary came to claim her more as patient than nurse. "My job is to be sick," she said.

Suffering became the rule for Sister Marie-Bernard. It also became prayer and penance, the substance of what Our Lady had asked of her. By late 1878, not long after she made her final profession, she was confined to her "white chapel," a white-curtained bed in Holy Cross Infirmary. Chronic asthma and coughing, spitting up of blood, the unrelenting pain of a tumor on her knee, chest pains, bedsores and abscesses all contributed to the sufferings, which Sister Marie-Bernard united with those of Christ.

During Holy Week of 1879, her pain escalated. "I'm being ground down like a grain of wheat," the miller's daughter said to a sister on Easter Monday. "I wouldn't have thought it took so much suffering to die."[5]

More was yet asked. Finally, on Easter Wednesday, April 16, Sister Marie-Bernard stretched out her arms like a cross and cried, "My God!" She joined in prayer with the other sisters present. "Holy Mary, Mother of God, pray for me a poor sinner," she repeated twice. After taking a few sips of water, Sister Marie-Bernard, whom the Blessed Mother could promise to make happy not in this world but in the other, died at the age of thirty-five.

Bernadette was beatified on June 14, 1925, and canonized in Rome on December 8, 1933—the Feast of the Immaculate Conception. Her incorrupt body rests in the chapel of the Convent of the Sisters of Charity in Nevers.

The pilgrims who follow in Bernadette's footsteps must also leave Lourdes, and many leave changed. In heeding the Blessed Virgin's call to penance and prayer, pilgrims must die to self. They find themselves humbled by the graces and healings received and perhaps more accepting of hopes denied.

"You're touched by God. Your life starts to reflect that, and that's contagious," says Father Clinton Zadroga, reflecting on the pilgrimages he has made. "Our being touched by God is going to have a small but still significant impact on people we relate to every day."

Completing the pilgrimage to Lourdes gave Tom Joyce the springboard he needed to deepen his commitment to Jesus Christ. "Undertaken sincerely, every personal pilgrimage should lead one to be just a bit more like Christ, strengthened for the journey of life and empowered to live one's baptism to the full," he says. While he experienced an immediate shot of spiritual adrenaline at Lourdes, Tom says that pilgrims might not recognize this spiritual boost instantly. "Some are gifted with an awareness of this before they leave. Some realize it upon returning home. Still others may only realize it as they look back on life," he believes.

"Regardless of our feelings, it is by its fruit that a tree is known. The real 'fruit' of a Lourdes pilgrimage is experienced by the way we live our lives on our return." Having journeyed to Lourdes, pilgrims are better equipped to reset their life compasses. "Yes, we'll have our human failings along the way, but we'll have rediscovered the way home to the Promised Land—Jesus Christ," Tom adds.

Other individuals who traveled to Lourdes expressed similar feelings after their return. Among them was Ellen McMahon, who served in the baths at Lourdes as a student volunteer. "When I think back on Lourdes now, I realize that I felt the closest to God when I was there. Lourdes makes me think of 'home,' because your ultimate home is with your Love and your Savior. When I think of Lourdes, I think of heaven. That was a taste of heaven for me," she recalls.

Some pilgrims returning from Lourdes notice changes in their prayer lives. Joan Straka cannot remember a time when prayer was not an important part of the rhythm of her daily life. As a child growing up in Chicago and then Omaha, she prayed the rosary daily with her family and on her bus ride to school. She remembers "block rosaries," when families gathered in neighbors' homes to pray for peace. In a way, Joan, her family and her neighbors lived prayer out loud in those times.

Joan recounts that at Lourdes she found a new way to pray. After the candlelight procession she and a small group of companions visited a chapel on their way back to the hotel. As they knelt in prayer before the tabernacle, Joan found that the uneasiness she sometimes experienced in meditating had vanished. Instead of wondering, as she often had, about the mechanics—for example, should she read a prayer book or try to reflect on Jesus—she found herself engaged in an intimate conversation.

"I just had a conversation with God. I just talked the way I'm talking to you," she remembers. "I thought, 'Oh, this is how it's supposed to be!' When I think about that whole trip to Lourdes, I think especially about that night and the significance of it for me."

Louise Sutton, a self-described "talker by nature," says it was always easy for her to pray alone or with others using words. "It was at Lourdes that I discovered the prayer of silence," she says. Her first experience of this came shortly after leaving the baths, when a sense of peace surrounded her. "We always are telling God everything he knows about us. It's important that we be still, know that he is God and ask him to speak to our hearts," she says. Since returning from Lourdes, Louise continues to listen to God in the quiet. "It is both healing and gift," she says.

For Father Clinton Zadroga, Our Lady of Lourdes seems more present to him in his prayer life now that he has visited the grotto. "Because of my pilgrimages to Lourdes and how intense those experiences were, now when I pray my rosary, when I offer some prayer to Our Lady, when I think of her, more often than not it's the image of the grotto and how she appeared there that's in my heart and in my mind," he says.

Katie Orbon—who went on pilgrimage with her husband, prayed for a baby and was blessed with a healthy son—stands in awe of the way her prayer life has changed since returning. When Katie went to Lourdes, she says, she was "not a very Marian person." That changed.

"It was amazing to me, sitting in the grotto at night, that you could feel her presence there. I had such a strong sense of her as a mom and how she could help me to be a good mom," Katie remembers. "It sounds so basic now, so obvious, but I was overwhelmed. It was overwhelming that I wanted to be where the Blessed Mother is." Katie prays the rosary more regularly now, asks for more in her prayers of intercession and appreciates the relationship she enjoys with Mary, her mother.

Howard Harrell, known as Pancho to his fellow North American Lourdes Volunteers, converted to Catholicism twenty-six years ago. He says his relationship with Mary was respectful but distant. On the feast day of the Immaculate Conception a few years ago, he began a novena asking Mary to help him know her better. Never did the restaurant manager from Texas dream that, within a year, he would volunteer at Lourdes and through that experience "meet" the Mother of God.

Assisting those on stretchers at the train station, Pancho met another volunteer, Vittorio Micheli, who had been cured completely of a sarcoma years earlier after bathing in the waters of the spring. If seeing a living miracle were not enough, Pancho points to an even greater blessing he experienced later. Standing on the platform of the station, he felt driven to visit the chapel there.

"I burst through the doors, broke out in tears, fell to my knees and prayed," Pancho recalls. "I looked down on the bench in front of me and saw nickel- and dime-size drops of tears." In that moment, he says, he encountered Mary in a way that words don't easily explain. Since then he's had a "true sense that Mary's watching over me," confirmed by events in his own life and the lives of the members of his family.

Alley LeStrange of Florida also has entered into a deeper devotion to Mary. A senior in high school, Alley is a Lourdes veteran. She has made five pilgrimages to the shrine in the company of the North American Lourdes Volunteers. Initially reluctant to go with her youth group, Alley's life was turned around by her first pilgrimage. She came home so on fire for Christ that she petitioned her bishop for early confirmation.

Each time Alley goes to Lourdes, she returns changed. This year, she says, she grew in her rosary devotion and her appreciation for the Mass. She spent a lot of time in the grotto praying. "I felt such a closeness with Mary, our mother," she recalls. "How great it is to know that we have a spiritual mother who will never fail us and who will lead us to her Son."

Julie Wlotzko, a student volunteer, wears a rosary bracelet, which she brought home from Lourdes. It's something tangible to remind her of what she experienced at Lourdes and how it changed her prayer life.

"What Lourdes taught me," Julie says, "is to look at another and see the face of Christ." She envisions the many women she served in the baths. "They were stripped of everything but the beautiful gift that God had made them," Julie remembers.

"Serving at Lourdes affected my prayer," she says. "You come to the realization that you encounter Christ in the everyday person." We can meet Christ not only through prayer and reflection but also in the person who stands beside us.

For Cora Sullivan, going to Lourdes impacted the frequency of her prayer. "I keep bothering the Blessed Mother more," Cora says. Distance poses no problem for Cora. Back home, four thousand miles from the grotto, she is within easy reach of Our Lady of Lourdes. "Even at night, if I can't sleep, I think of Lourdes. I'm in the grotto. I'm looking at the statue of the Blessed Mother. It gives me peace. If I can't go to sleep, in my mind I just transfer myself back to Lourdes."

A fellow pilgrim, Kathleen Gallagher, agrees. "I love Our Lady. I know she's with me if I'm at the grotto or wherever I am, but I can put myself back at the grotto like that," Kathleen says, snapping her fingers. "I can close down and be there in my mind."

Pilgrims often ask Father Régis-Marie de La Teyssonnière, Chaplain of Honor of Our Lady of Lourdes, how they might continue the experience of Lourdes at home. "The answer is easy," he says. "If you really experienced Lourdes one time, you will not be able to forget the experience. The Lourdes experience is a spiritual experience in a very concrete context. What is spiritual has no borders."

Father de La Teyssonnière recommends as the model Bernadette, who loved and missed her grotto. "She left Lourdes eight years after the apparitions to enter the Convent of St. Gildard in Nevers, where she remained to the end of her life, thirteen years later," he explains. "Several times Bernadette revealed her secret, saying, 'Every day I go in pilgrimage to the grotto.'"

What this suggests to today's pilgrims, Father de La Teyssonnière believes, is that it's possible to revisit Lourdes without ever leaving home. "Every day Bernadette went in the deepest place of her heart, where she encountered Our Lady, her Son, Jesus, and the friends of Jesus, all the saints," says Father de La Teyssonnière. "To make the spiritual journey, her knowledge of the grotto was very helpful to her," he adds. "Closing her eyes, she was able to imagine the grotto and be in the same experience as when she was there, in the same experience of her last 'visit' to the grotto, the day before."

For the millions of people who have never been in Lourdes, Father de La Teyssonnière believes the opportunity to experience the grace of that place is within easy reach. He recommends looking at a picture or postcard of the grotto. Just as gazing at a crèche or the cross helps Christians prayerfully reflect on our Lord's incarnation or his death, looking at an image of the grotto shortens the distance between our meditation and the graces of the holy shelter.

What possible meaning does the message of Lourdes have for the world today, a world 150 years removed from the apparitions of the Blessed Mother?

For many the message of Lourdes speaks of the importance of assessing what we have placed first in our lives. Father Clinton Zadroga believes it is a message that counters our misplaced priorities, in which we measure success by what we own, what positions we hold or what standard of living we achieve. "More than ever we need to be saved from that illusion that this world and this life is it. Our Lady of Lourdes—from that holy place—is telling us that there is so much more. The love of Jesus is more real than this passing world," says Father Clint.

Dr. Michael Martinelli thinks along those same lines. "We can get so bound by the world, so busy, so involved in things of the world, that we lose sight of what's really important," he says. Neglecting our prayer life and not realizing that our spiritual house is paramount, Dr. Martinelli believes, "does great damage to our souls by turning us away from God." The call to prayer and penance issued by Our Lady in the Grotto of Massabielle helps to redirect our focus.

Father de La Teyssonnière underscores the same. "Our world is not the goal of life—just the door to enter the other world," he says.

Tom Joyce frames the value of Lourdes in the context of today's world and its condition. "Are we any healthier, any less bankrupt, any less dysfunctional, than at any other time in history? We're extremely dysfunctional. We're extremely divided. We're extremely broken," he observes. "We're extremely in need of healing. Who else can bring that about but our Lord? And who else but Mary can bring this entire canopy under her mantle and bring us to her Son?

"Do we need it now? Do we need Lourdes? Absolutely! The question is, how can we do without it? We can't."

Student Julie Wlotzko interprets what happened in the grotto 150 years ago and what has happened since as "radical." It should challenge our complacency, she says. In today's culture, Julie believes, it's easy to dismiss what can't be explained or proven through science. "It's not logical that you can step into a bath and be healed or that the Eucharist can heal a person physically, spiritually or emotionally," she says. Lourdes, with its history of miracles, cures and conversions, defies logic and teaches believers to have expectant faith. "Expectant faith is what keeps us moving. Expectant faith keeps our eyes focused on Christ," Julie says. "And that's really when the healing can take place."

Sister Anne Marie Gill, T.O.R., assistant director of evangelization at Franciscan University of Steubenville, accompanies pilgrimages with the North American Lourdes Volunteers. She believes that the message of Lourdes cannot be more relevant or more critical. The heart of the New Evangelization, spoken of by Pope John Paul II and then Cardinal Joseph Ratzinger, the future Pope Benedict XVI, is not a new message but a call for a relationship between God and man. "It's about encountering a living Christ. It's having a living relationship with Jesus. The world desperately needs people to know Christ," Sister Anne Marie says. "You can teach concepts, but unless they encounter the living person, Jesus Christ, who poured himself out in love for us, the words of the gospel mean nothing."

In addressing catechists and religion teachers on the call to the New Evangelization, Cardinal Ratzinger spoke of this relationship. He simplified the message of Christianity to a handful of words. "We speak about God and man, and this way we say everything," he concluded.[6]

Lourdes builds or repairs this relationship between God and his children. "Everything about Lourdes is Mary saying, 'Do whatever he tells you,'" Sister Anne Marie says.

"It's Mary pointing back to her Son. Every element of Lourdes encourages you to know him in a personal way. It is the heart of the gospel: repent and believe the good news that Christ is Lord."

The jubilee years of the past—both the golden and centenary anniversaries of the apparitions—introduced something new, something life-giving, to Lourdes. In 1908 pontifical high Masses commemorated the fiftieth anniversary of the first (February 11) and the last (July 16) apparitions of Our Lady to Bernadette. Members of Bernadette's family attended, as did Jeanne Abadie, who with

Toinette Soubirous accompanied Bernadette to the grotto the day the Blessed Virgin first appeared. Cardinal Roncalli, the future Pope John XXIII, came to Lourdes during the 100th jubilee to consecrate the Basilica of St. Pius X. The authorized story of the apparitions written by Marian scholar Father René Laurentin was introduced.

But for the 150th anniversary, Bishop Jacques Perrier posed this question: What can Lourdes do to proclaim the gospel today? As Bernadette always looked to be useful in her religious life, Lourdes too seeks to be useful in new ways. Beyond the festive celebrations of the golden anniversary, beyond the building and books distinguishing the centenary anniversary and beyond the traditional pilgrimages that have bridged all the years of its history, what can Lourdes do in this third millennium?

It is in the spirit of the New Evangelization, Bishop Perrier believes, that Lourdes can best celebrate the 150th anniversary of the apparitions and move ahead in drawing more people to Christ. In its anniversary program, the Sanctuary of Our Lady of Lourdes signals a new direction for the future. "Lourdes is like a field of wheat," it begins. "The field fed many generations. But it is now ready for a new harvest."[7]

Lourdes is ready for new missions in order to further proclaim the gospel in words and actions to the millions who come to drink, draw strength and wash in the little spring. Twelve missions--each rooted in the New Testament and each paired with one or more large pilgrimage groups—are planned to draw visitors and to emphasize the Church's role in the world.

Lourdes will highlight during the 150th Jubilee Year the Church's mission nourished by the *Eucharist* ("I am the Bread of

Life") and accompanied by *Mary* ("Behold your mother"); its mission to the *world* ("Men of every race, language, people and nation") and for *peace* ("Peace to men whom God loves"); and its mission to those who require the care and concern of others, including the *sick* ("I was sick and you visited me"), the *handicapped* ("He saw a man blind from birth") and the *marginalized* ("He saw a man sitting by the roadside").

Additionally, Lourdes will recognize the Church's commitment to *Christian unity* ("That they may all be one") and *interreligious dialogue* ("Before him will be gathered all the nations"). The mission of the Church in *service to others* ("Not to be served but to serve") and in transforming hearts through *conversion* ("Repent, the kingdom of God is at hand") will also be addressed. The final mission of the Church regards its future, that is, its mission to *young people* ("Young man, I say to you, get up").[8]

Lourdes welcomes pilgrims with interests corresponding to the distinctive missions to come when these are celebrated, to join in the discussions and participate in the events. These missions represent a departure from and are in addition to the usual activities at Lourdes. They may be the soil upon which Lourdes grows initiatives for the future. In an interview published in *Lourdes Magazine*, Bishop Perrier said, "The advantage of the jubilee year is that it is an exception. If something new succeeds, very well. It can give ideas for the future. If it fails, it does not matter: 'It was for the jubilee year!' But, in fact, nothing ever fails in Lourdes."[9]

Though maybe, given the spirit of the New Evangelization, success might not be immediately—if ever—determined. Cardinal Ratzinger, five years before being elected pope, warned of "impatience, the temptation of immediately finding the great success, in finding large numbers" to judge the effectiveness of the New Evangelization. The parable of the mustard seed holds true, he said, both for the kingdom of God and the outreach on which it is built. The New Evangelization, he concludes, "means to dare, once again and with the humility of the small grain, to leave up to God the when and how it will grow (Mark 4:26–29)."[10]

This lesson Lourdes knows well. Bernadette Soubirous, the sickly, uneducated fourteen-year-old daughter of a failed miller, knelt in prayer 150 years ago in a desolate rock shelter. More than 300,000,000 people have followed in her footsteps along the pilgrim way to a deeper knowledge and love of the Blessed Virgin and her Son.

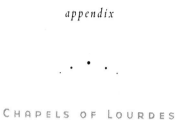

CHAPELS OF LOURDES

There are more than twenty places of worship in the Sanctuary of Our Lady of Lourdes. These are among the most visited.

THE CRYPT

The Crypt was the first chapel built in answer to Our Lady's request to Bernadette, "Go, tell the priests to have a chapel built here." Designed by M. Hippolyte Durand, construction began in 1862, four years after the apparitions. François Soubirous, Bernadette's father, numbered among the local laborers who helped build it. Bishop Laurence dedicated the Crypt on May 19, 1866, the Vigil of Pentecost, with Bernadette in attendance.

Ex-voto offerings—marble tablets engraved with prayers of thanksgiving for favors received—line the walls of the long entrance corridor. Once inside, pilgrims' eyes are drawn to the altar, above which a statue of the Blessed Virgin and the child Jesus is mounted, surrounded by golden rays. Fabisch, the artist who sculpted the grotto statue of Our Lady of Lourdes, created this statue.

An altar dedicated to Saint Joseph is on the right side of the chapel. During Eucharistic adoration pilgrims worship Jesus in the monstrance that Pope John Paul II gave to Lourdes. The intimate chapel seats slightly more than 100 pilgrims.

THE BASILICA OF THE IMMACULATE CONCEPTION

The Basilica of the Immaculate Conception, or the upper basilica, was built above the Crypt between 1866 and 1872. Pope Pius IX raised it to the rank of a minor basilica in 1874. With its 230-foot main spire, the basilica dominates the Domain as well as the valleys surrounding it. It seats 550 people.

As pilgrims enter the basilica, they find to their right a marble plaque containing the complete text of Bishop Laurence's judgment of the validity of the apparitions. Stained glass windows in this single-nave church tell the story of the Blessed Virgin, concluding with Saint Pius IX's declaration of the dogma of the Immaculate Conception (1854) and the apparitions (1858). The altar is directly above where the Blessed Virgin appeared to Bernadette. As in the Crypt, ex-voto offerings reveal the gratitude of past pilgrims for Our Lady's intercession.

THE ROSARY BASILICA

The Rosary Basilica was added to accommodate 1,500 pilgrims. Leopold Hardy designed the church, which was built between 1883 and 1889, consecrated in 1901 and raised to a minor basilica in 1926. It extends in front of the Basilica of the Immaculate Conception and the Crypt.

A gold crown and a cross cap the outer dome of the basilica. Over the entrance is a relief of the Blessed Virgin and the child Jesus offering a rosary to Saint Dominic. Inside, the nave is surrounded by fifteen side chapels. Each depicts in mosaics the mysteries of the rosary—to the left, the Joyful Mysteries; behind the Sanctuary, the Sorrowful Mysteries; and to the right, the Glorious Mysteries. Mosaics of the Luminous Mysteries are planned in honor of John Paul II.

THE BASILICA OF ST. PIUS X

Architect Pierre Vargo designed this building to accommodate the crowds for the 100th anniversary of the apparitions. One of the largest churches in the world, it seats 25,000 pilgrims. The oval nave measures 626 by 200 feet.

The coldness of the concrete construction is offset somewhat by the nonleaded stained glass panels created in the local Gemmail style, in which glass pieces overlap to create intensity in color shadings and light. The panels depict the Stations of the Cross, the mysteries of the rosary and the apparitions of Lourdes.

Large banners of holy men and women also brighten the basilica. Among those represented are saints and blesseds of recent years, including Saint Edith Stein, Saint Pio de Pietrelcina, Saint Josemariá Escrivá, Blessed Mother Teresa of Calcutta, Blessed Mother Marianne Cope and Blessed John XXIII. It was John XXIII, as Cardinal Roncalli, who consecrated the underground basilica in 1958. International Masses are held here twice a week, and the blessing of the sick every day during pilgrimage season.

THE CHURCH OF ST. BERNADETTE

Located opposite the grotto and across the River Gave, the Church of St. Bernadette rests near the spot where Bernadette prayed on July 16, 1858, the evening of the final apparition. Jean-Paul Felix designed this church built of metal and concrete and consecrated in 1988.

A large icon of Our Lady of Cambrai, an image some say Bernadette once likened to the Blessed Virgin in the grotto, hangs in the Sanctuary. The church seats 5,000, with additional space for 300 in wheelchairs or on stretchers.

CHAPEL OF RECONCILIATION

The Chapel of Reconciliation, dedicated exclusively to the celebration of the sacrament of penance, is located to the right of the Statue of the Crowned Virgin.

THE TENT OF ADORATION

The Tent of Adoration was placed on the prairie near the lower bridge in 2001. Pilgrims who wish to spend time in prayer before the Blessed Sacrament during the day gather under its canopy.

THE ADORATION CHAPEL

The Adoration Chapel, blessed and opened in 1995, features three biblical symbols. The cloth on the ceiling signifies the tent of meeting. The gilded column of wood symbolizes the cloud of fire that led the Israelites across the desert to the Promised Land. It contains the tabernacle for the Eucharist, Christ, who leads his people now. The twelve columns in the chapel honor the twelve apostles, representing the New Jerusalem. Designed by Paul Félix, the building is shaped like a tent.

NOTES

CHAPTER ONE: BERNADETTE AND THE LADY

1. Letter of Bernadette Soubirous, May 28, 1861, in *Lourdes Magazine,* June/July 2005, p. 4.

2. Patricia A. McEachern, *A Holy Life: The Writings of Saint Bernadette of Lourdes* (San Francisco: Ignatius, 2005), p. 206.

3. "Diary of the Apparitions," *Lourdes Magazine,* June/July 2005, p. 26.

4. René Laurentin, *Bernadette Speaks: A Life of Saint Bernadette Soubirous in Her Own Words,* John W. Lynch and Ronald DesRosiers, trans. (Boston: Pauline, 2000), p. 46. Much of the history of Bernadette, the apparitions and her life as a religious in Nevers is based on this.

5. "Diary of the Apparitions."

6. "Diary of the Apparitions."

7. Laurentin, p. 57

8. "Diary of the Apparitions."

9. "Diary of the Apparitions."

10. Laurentin, p. 108.

11. McEachern, p. 212.

12. "The Church Officially Recognises the Apparitions," www.lourdes-france.org.

CHAPTER TWO: MIRACLES, CURES AND BLESSINGS

1. Matthias Terrier and updated by Laurent Jarneau, "The Miraculous Cures of Lourdes," *Lourdes Magazine,* Special Edition: "Cures and Miracles," pp. 11–31. Profiles of *miraculés* in this chapter are based on this article. The first *miraculée* given in this source is more frequently identified as Catherine Latapie-Chouat.

2. "The Church Officially Recognises the Apparitions."

3. Franz Werfel, a Jewish Viennese novelist, found refuge at Lourdes when fleeing National Socialists and vowed to write the story of Bernadette once he arrived in America. See Franz Werfel, *The Song of Bernadette*, trans. Ludwig Lewisohn (San Francisco: Ignatius, 2006).

4. "Statistics on the 67 Miraculous Cures of Lourdes," *Lourdes Magazine*, Special Edition: 5. "Cures and Miracles," p. 32.

5. Jacques Perrier, "Today's Position on 'Miracles'," *Lourdes Magazine*, Special Edition: "Cures and Miracles," pp. 2–3.

6. "The Church Officially Recognises the Apparitions."

CHAPTER THREE: EVERYDAY PILGRIMS

1. Joseph Cardinal Ratizinger, *Behold the Pierced One*, trans. Graham Harrison (San Francisco: Ignatius, 1986), p. 107.

2. Pontifical Council for the Pastoral Care of Migrants, "The Pilgrimage in the Great Jubilee," April 1998, no. 2, www.vatican.va.

3. Letter from Father James R. Cox to Bishop Hugh C. Boyle, July 14, 1947, Diocese of Pittsburgh Archives.

4. Sally Witt, "From the Ranks of the Ordinary People: Father Cox and Pittsburgh in the 1940s," *Pittsburgh History*, vol. 80, no. 2 (Summer 1997), p. 55.

5. Laurent Jarneau and Mathias Terrier, "A People from Every Nation in Lourdes," *Lourdes Magazine*, October/November 2002, pp. 32–33.

6. "Popes and Lourdes," www.lourdes-france.org.

7. "Dublin Diocesan Pilgrimage to Lourdes," http://lourdes.t73.nuahost.com.

8. Introduction of the Holy Father John Paul II to the Torchlight Procession, Accueil Notre-Dame, August 14, 2004, no. 1.

9. Quoted in Nicole Chareyon, *Pilgrims to Jerusalem in the Middle Ages* (New York: Columbia University Press, 2005), p. 16.

CHAPTER FOUR: THE SICK AND SUFFERING

1. Message of John Paul II to the Faith and Light Movement, no. 5, April 2, 2001, www.vatican.va.

2. John Paul II, *Salvifici Doloris*, Apostolic Letter on the Christian Meaning of Human Suffering, no. 26, February 11, 1984, www.vatican.va.

3. *Salvifici Doloris*, no. 30.

4. John Paul II, *A Pilgrim Pope: Messages for the World*, Cardinal Achille Silvestrini

and Jerome M. Vereb, eds. (New York: Gramercy, 2004), p. 82.

5. *A Pilgrim Pope*, p. 83.

6. Thomas Rosica, "John Paul II's Master Class to His 'Dear Young Friends,'" talk given to University of Toronto Catholic Community, April 4, 2005.

7. Greeting of John Paul II to the Sick, August 14, 2004, www.vatican.va.

8. Message of the Holy Father John Paul II for the First Annual World Day of the Sick, no. 6, October 21, 1992, www.vatican.va.

9. Message of His Holiness John Paul II for the Twelfth World Day of the Sick, no. 3, December 3, 2003.

CHAPTER FIVE: HOSPITALITY

1. Best Western.

2. *Salvifici Doloris*, no. 16.

3. *Salvifici Doloris*, no. 28

CHAPTER SIX: ROCK

1. "In the Footsteps of Bernadette," www.lourdes-france.org.

2. Details about Lourdes, its workforce, places to visit and statistics are from the official Lourdes Internet site, www.lourdes-france.org.

3. "G...for Grotto," Message of Lourdes: Letter for the 150th Anniversary of the Apparitions, *Lourdes Magazine*, 2006, www.lourdes-france.com.

4. "G...for Grotto."

5. Benedict XVI, Angelus, February 11, 2007.

6. John Paul II, Homily, Lourdes, August 15, 2004, no. 7, www.vatican.va.

7. John Paul II, Homily, August 15, 2004, no. 5

CHAPTER SEVEN: WATER

1. "Good-Bye to John Paul II: Selection of Words of John Paul II in Lourdes in 1983," www.lourdes-france.org.

2. Jacques Perrier, "My Soul Is Thirsting for the Living God," *Lourdes Magazine*, October/November 2001, pp. 6–9.

3. "The Water of the Spring," www.lourdes-france.org.

4. René Point, "An Act of Magic?" *Lourdes Magazine*, October/November 2001, p. 51.

5. Laurentin, p. 187.

6. John Paul II, Angelus, Lourdes, August 15, 2004, www.vatican.va.

7. "A Path and Nine Wells," *The Water Walk* (Lourdes: NDL Editions), pp. 1–13.

8. Perrier, p. 8.

9. "Meeting Basic Needs," World Water Assessment Program, www.unesco.org/water/wwap.

10. Homily of His Holiness Benedict XVI, Inauguration of the Pontificate, St. Peter's Square, April 24, 2005, www.vatican.va.

11. Benedict XVI, *Deus Caritas Est*, Encyclical Letter on Christian Love, no. 42, December 25, 2005, vatican.va.

CHAPTER EIGHT: LIGHT

1. André Doze, "What Is the Origin of the Torchlight Procession?" *Lourdes Magazine*, October/November 2005, p. 20.

2. Introduction of the Holy Father John Paul II to the Torchlight Procession, Accueil Notre-Dame, August 14, 2004.

3. Benedict XVI, "On the Rosary and Missions," Angelus, October 1, 2006 (Vatican: Libreria Editrice Vaticana, 2006).

4. John Paul II, *Rosarium Virginis Mariae*, Apostolic Letter on the Most Holy Rosary, no. 14, October 16, 2002, www.vatican.va.

5. "Pope John Paul II, Torchlight Marian Procession / Pastoral Theme," August 14, 1983, www.lourdes-france.

6. United States Conference of Catholic Bishops, Committee on the Liturgy, "The New Missale Romanum and the Easter Vigil," March 14, 2006, www.usccb.org.

7. Laurent Jarneau, "Guardian Angels of the Fire," *Lourdes Magazine*, October/November 2005, pp. 37, 40.

8. *Way of the Cross* (Lourdes: Sanctuaires Notre-Dame de Lourdes).

9. John Paul II, *Mane Nobiscum Domine*, Apostolic Letter for the Year of the Eucharist, no. 11, October 2004–2005, www.vatican.va.

10. *Mane Nobiscum Domine*, no. 2.

11. Benedict XVI, *Sacramentum Caritas*, Post-Synodal Apostolic Exortation on the Eucharist as the Source and Summit of the Church's Life and Mission, no. 97, February 22, 2007, www.vatican.va.

CHAPTER NINE: WHEAT

1. Laurentin, p. 310.

2. Laurentin, p. 340.

3. Joseph Bordes, *Lourdes: In Bernadette's Footsteps*, John Lochran, trans. (Cedex, France: MSM, 2005), p. 47.

4. Laurentin, p. 330.

5. Laurentin, p. 525.

6. Joseph Cardinal Ratzinger, "The New Evangelization," The Jubilee of Catechists, 2000, www.tcrnew2.com.

7. "The Twelve Missions of Lourdes for Today," 150th Anniversary of the Apparitions Programme, *Lourdes Magazine* insert, December 2007/January 2008.

8. "Lourdes: bientôt 150 years" [Lourdes: almost 150 years], press dossier provided by Sanctuaires Notre-Dame de Lourdes, Paris, March 16, 2006.

9. "Towards an 'Exceptional Year,'" interview with Bishop Jacques Perrier, *Lourdes Magazine* insert, December 2006/January 2007, p. ii.

10. Ratzinger, "The New Evangelization."